deceived, a play is supposed to be the work of the poet, imitating, or representing, the conversation of several persons: and this I think to be as clear, as he thinks the contrary.

But I will be bolder, and do not doubt to make it good, though a paradox, that one great reason why prose is not to be used in serious plays, is, because it is too near the nature of converse: There may be too great a likeness; as the most skilful painters affirm, that there may be too near a resemblance in a picture: To take every lineament and feature is not to make an excellent piece, but to take so much only as will make a beautiful resemblance of the whole: and, with an ingenious flattery of nature, to heighten the beauties of some parts, and hide the deformities of the rest. For so says Horace,

Ut pictura poesis erit. &c. —
Haec amat obscurum, vult haec sub luce videri,
Judicis argutum quae formidat acumen.
Et quae
Desperat tractata nitescere posse, relinquit.

In "Bartholomew Fair," or the lowest kind of comedy, that degree of heightening is used, which is proper to set off that subject: It is true the author was not there to go out of prose, as he does in his higher arguments of comedy, "The Fox" and "Alchemist;" yet he does so raise his matter in that prose, as to render it delightful; which he could never have performed, had he only said or done those very things, that are daily spoken or practised in the fair: for then the fair itself would be as full of pleasure to an ingenious person as the play, which we manifestly see it is not. But he hath made an excellent lazar of it; the copy is of price, though the original be vile. You see in "Catiline" and "Sejanus," where the argument is great, he sometimes ascends to verse, which shews he thought it not unnatural in serious plays; and had his genius been as proper for rhyme as it was for humour, or had the age in which he lived attained to as much knowledge in verse as ours, it is probable he would have adorned those subjects with that kind of writing.

Thus Prose, though the rightful prince, yet is by common consent deposed, as too weak for the government of serious plays: and he failing, there now start up two competitors; one, the nearer in blood, which is Blank Verse; the other, more fit for the ends of government, which is Rhyme. Blank Verse is, indeed, the nearer Prose, but he is blemished with the weakness of his predecessor. Rhyme (for I will deal clearly) has somewhat of the usurper in him; but he is brave, and generous, and his dominion pleasing. For this reason of delight, the ancients (whom I will still believe as wise as those who so confidently correct them) wrote all their tragedies in verse, though they knew it most remote from conversation.

But I perceive I am falling into the danger of another rebuke from my opponent; for when I plead that the ancients used verse, I prove not that they would have admitted rhyme, had it then been written. All I can say is only this, that it seems to have succeeded verse by the general consent of poets in all modern languages; for almost all their serious plays are written in it; which, though it be no demonstration that therefore they ought to be so, yet at least the practice first, and then the continuation of it, shews that it attained the end, which was to please; and if that cannot be compassed here, I will be the first who shall lay it down: for I confess my chief endeavours are to delight the age in which I live. If the humour of this be for low comedy, small accidents, and raillery, I will force my genius to obey it, though with more reputation I could write in verse. I know I am not so fitted by nature to write comedy: I want that gaiety of humour which is required to it. My conversation is slow and dull; my humour saturnine and reserved: In short, I am none of those who endeavour to break jests in company, or make repartees. So that those, who decry my comedies, do me no injury, except it be in point of profit: reputation in them is the last thing to which I shall pretend. I beg pardon for entertaining the reader with so ill a subject; but before I quit that argument, which was the cause of this digression, I cannot but take notice how I am corrected for my quotation of Seneca, in my defence of plays in verse. My words are these: "Our language is noble, full, and significant; and I know not why he, who is a master of, it, may not clothe ordinary things in it as decently as in the Latin, if he use the same diligence in his choice of words." One would think, "unlock a door," was a thing as vulgar as could be spoken; yet Seneca could make it sound high and lofty in his Latin.

"Reserate clusos regii postes laris."

But he says of me, "That being filled with the precedents of the ancients, who writ their plays in verse, I commend the thing, declaring our language to be full, noble, and significant, and charging all defects upon the ill placing of words, which I prove by quoting Seneca loftily expressing such an ordinary thing as shutting a door."

Here he manifestly mistakes; for I spoke not of the placing, but of the choice of words; for which I quoted that aphorism of Julius Caesar, Delectus verborum est origo eloquentiae; but delectus verborum is no more Latin for the placing of words, than reserate is Latin for shut the door, as he interprets it, which I ignorantly construed unlock or open it.

He supposes I was highly affected with the sound of those words, and I suppose I may more justly imagine it of him; for if he had not been extremely satisfied with the sound, he would have minded the sense a little better.

But these are now to be no faults; for ten days after his book is published, and that his mistakes are grown so famous, that they are come back to him, he sends his Errata[A] to be printed, and annexed to his play; and desires, that, instead of shutting, you would read opening, which, it seems, was the printer's fault. I wonder at his modesty, that he did not rather say it was Seneca's or mine; and that, in some authors, reserate was to shut as well as to open, as the word barach, say the learned, is both to bless and curse.

[Footnote A: This erratum has been suffered to remain in the edition of the Knight's plays now before us, published in 1692.]

Well, since it was the printer, he was a naughty man to commit the same mistake twice in six lines: I warrant you delectus verborum, for placing of words, was his mistake too, though the author forgot to tell him of it: If it were my book, I assure you I should. For those rascals ought to be the proxies of every gentleman author, and to be chastised for him, when he is not pleased to own an error. Yet since he has given the errata, I wish he would have enlarged them only a few sheets more, and then he would have spared me the labour of an answer: For this cursed printer is so given to mistakes, that there is scarce a sentence in the preface without some false grammar, or hard sense in it; which will all be charged upon the poet, because he is so good-natured as to lay but three errors to the printer's account, and to take the rest upon himself, who is better able to support them. But he needs not apprehend that I should strictly examine those little faults, except I am called upon to do it: I shall return therefore to that quotation of Seneca, and answer, not to what he writes, but to what he means. I never intended it as an argument, but only as an illustration of what I had said before concerning the election of words; and all he can charge me with is only this, that if Seneca could make an ordinary thing sound well in Latin by the choice of words, the same, with the like care, might be performed in English: If it cannot, I have committed an error on the right hand, by commending too much the copiousness and well-sounding of our language, which I hope my countrymen will pardon me; at least the words which follow in my Dramatic Essay will plead

The Indian Emperor by John Dryden

John Dryden was born on August 9th, 1631 in the village rectory of Aldwincle near Thrapston in Northamptonshire. As a boy Dryden lived in the nearby village of Titchmarsh, Northamptonshire. In 1644 he was sent to Westminster School as a King's Scholar.

Dryden obtained his BA in 1654, graduating top of the list for Trinity College, Cambridge that year.

Returning to London during The Protectorate, Dryden now obtained work with Cromwell's Secretary of State, John Thurloe.

At Cromwell's funeral on 23 November 1658 Dryden was in the company of the Puritan poets John Milton and Andrew Marvell. The setting was to be a sea change in English history. From Republic to Monarchy and from one set of lauded poets to what would soon become the Age of Dryden.

The start began later that year when Dryden published the first of his great poems, Heroic Stanzas (1658), a eulogy on Cromwell's death.

With the Restoration of the Monarchy in 1660 Dryden celebrated in verse with Astraea Redux, an authentic royalist panegyric.

With the re-opening of the theatres after the Puritan ban, Dryden began to also write plays. His first play, The Wild Gallant, appeared in 1663 but was not successful. From 1668 on he was contracted to produce three plays a year for the King's Company, in which he became a shareholder. During the 1660s and '70s, theatrical writing was his main source of income.

In 1667, he published Annus Mirabilis, a lengthy historical poem which described the English defeat of the Dutch naval fleet and the Great Fire of London in 1666. It established him as the pre-eminent poet of his generation, and was crucial in his attaining the posts of Poet Laureate (1668) and then historiographer royal (1670).

This was truly the Age of Dryden, he was the foremost English Literary figure in Poetry, Plays, translations and other forms.

In 1694 he began work on what would be his most ambitious and defining work as translator, The Works of Virgil (1697), which was published by subscription. It was a national event.

John Dryden died on May 12th, 1700, and was initially buried in St. Anne's cemetery in Soho, before being exhumed and reburied in Westminster Abbey ten days later.

Index of Contents

INTRODUCTION AND PROLOGUE

TO THE MOST EXCELLENT AND MOST ILLUSTRIOUS PRINCESS, ANNE, DUCHESS OF MONMOUTH AND BUCCLEUCH, WIFE TO THE MOST ILLUSTRIOUS AND HIGH-BORN PRINCE, JAMES, DUKE OF MONMOUTH[A].

[A] Anne Scott, duchess of Buccleuch and Monmouth, was the last scion of a race of warriors, more remarkable for their exploits in the field, than their address in courts, or protection of literature. She was the heiress of the Scotts, barons and earls of Buccleuch; and became countess, in her own right, upon the death of her elder sister, lady Mary, who married the unfortunate Walter Scott, earl of Tarras, and died without issue in 1662. In 1665, Anne, countess of Buccleuch, married James Fitzroy, duke of Monmouth, eldest natural son of Charles II. They were afterwards created duke and duchess of Buccleuch. She was an accomplished and high-spirited lady, distinguished for her unblemished conduct in a profligate court. It was her patronage which first established Dryden's popularity; a circumstance too honourable to her memory to be here suppressed.]

May it please Your Grace,

The favour which heroic plays have lately found upon our theatres, has been wholly derived to them from the countenance and approbation they have received at court. The most eminent persons for wit and honour in the royal circle having so far owned them, that they have judged no way so fit as verse to entertain a noble audience, or to express a noble passion; and among the rest which have been written in this kind, they have been so indulgent to this poem, as to allow it no inconsiderable place. Since, therefore, to the court I owe its fortune on the stage; so, being now more publicly exposed in print, I humbly recommend it to your grace's protection, who by all knowing persons are esteemed a principal ornament of the court. But though the rank which you hold in the royal family might direct the eyes of a poet to you, yet your beauty and goodness detain and fix them. High objects, it is true, attract the sight; but it looks up with pain on craggy rocks and barren mountains, and continues not intent on any object, which is wanting in shades and greens to entertain it.

Beauty, in courts, is so necessary to the young, that those, who are without it, seem to be there to no other purpose than to wait on the triumphs of the fair; to attend their motions in obscurity, as the moon and stars do the sun by day; or, at best, to be the refuge of those hearts which others have despised; and, by the unworthiness of both, to give and take a miserable comfort. But as needful as beauty is, virtue and honour are yet more: The reign of it without their support is unsafe and short, like that of tyrants. Every sun which looks on beauty wastes it; and, when it once is decaying, the repairs of art are of as short continuance, as the after-spring, when the sun is going further off. This, madam, is its ordinary fate; but yours, which is accompanied by virtue, is not subject to that common destiny. Your grace has not only a long time of youth in which to flourish, but you have likewise found the way, by an untainted preservation of your honour, to make that perishable good more lasting: And if beauty, like wines, could be preserved, by being mixed and embodied with others of their own natures, then your grace's would be immortal, since no part of Europe can afford a parallel to your noble lord in masculine beauty, and in goodliness of shape. To receive the blessings and prayers of mankind, you need only to be seen together: We are ready to conclude, that you are a pair of angels sent below to make virtue amiable in your persons, or to sit to poets when they would pleasantly instruct the age, by drawing goodness in the most perfect and alluring shape of nature. But though beauty be the theme on which poets love to dwell, I must be forced to quit it as a private praise, since you have deserved those which are more public: For goodness and humanity, which shine in you, are virtues which concern mankind; and, by a certain kind of interest, all people agree in their commendation, because the profit of them may extend to many. It is so much your inclination to do good, that you stay not to be asked; which is an approach so nigh the Deity, that human nature is not capable of a nearer. It is my happiness, that I can testify this virtue of your grace's by my own experience; since I have so great an aversion from soliciting court-favours, that I am ready to look on those as very bold, who dare grow rich there without desert. But I beg your grace's pardon for assuming this virtue of modesty to myself, which the sequel of this discourse will no way justify: For in this address I have already quitted the character of a modest man, by presenting you this poem as an acknowledgment, which stands in need of your protection; and which ought no more to be esteemed a present, than it is accounted bounty in the poor, when they bestow a child on some wealthy friend, who will better breed it up. Offsprings of this nature are like to be so numerous with me, that I must be forced to send some of them abroad; only this is like to be more fortunate than his brothers, because I have landed him on a hospitable shore.

Under your patronage Montezuma hopes he is more safe than in his native Indies; and therefore comes to throw himself at your grace's feet, paying that homage to your beauty, which he refused to the violence of his conquerors. He begs only, that when he shall relate his sufferings, you will consider him as an Indian Prince, and not expect any other eloquence from his simplicity, than what his griefs have furnished him withal. His story is, perhaps, the greatest which was ever represented in a poem of this nature; the action of it including the discovery and conquest of a new world. In it I have neither wholly followed the truth of the history, nor altogether left it; but have taken all the liberty of a poet, to add, alter, or diminish, as I thought might best conduce to the beautifying of my work: it being not the business of a poet to represent historical truth, but probability. But I am not to make the justification of this poem, which I wholly leave to your grace's mercy. It is an irregular piece, if compared with many of Corneille's, and, if I may make a judgment of it, written with more flame than art; in which it represents the mind and intentions of the author, who is with much more zeal and integrity, than design and artifice,

MADAM,
Your Grace's most obedient,
And most obliged servant,
JOHN DRYDEN,
October 12. 1667.

Betwixt 1664, when our author assisted Sir Robert Howard in composing the preceding play, and the printing of the Indian Emperor in 1668, some disagreement had arisen betwixt them. Sir Robert appears to have given the first provocation, by prefixing to his tragedy of the Duke of Lerma, or Great Favourite, in 1668, some remarks, which drew down the following severe retort. It is therefore necessary to mention the contents of the offensive preface.

Sir Robert Howard begins, as one taking leave of the drama and dramatic authors, "his too long acquaintances;" and unwilling again to venture "into the civil wars of Censure,

Ubi—Nullos habitura triumphos."

He states his unwilling interference to be owing to the "unnecessary understanding" of some, who endeavoured to apply as strict rules to poetry as mathematics, which rendered it incumbent on him to justify his having written some scenes of his tragedy in blank verse. In the next paragraph, Dryden is expressly pointed out as the author of the Essay on Dramatic Poetry; and is ridiculed for attempting to prove, not that rhyme is more natural in a dialogue on the stage supposed to be spoken extempore, but grander and more expressive. In like manner, Sir Robert unfortunately banters our author for drawing from Seneca an instance of a lofty mode of expressing so ordinary a thing as shutting a door[A], instead of giving an example to the same effect in English.

[Footnote A:

Reserate clusos regii postes laris.
Howard's mistranslation of this passage seems to have been inadvertent. In the Essay it is rendered, "Set wide the palace gates."]

The author of the Duke of Lerma proceeds to attack the unities; arguing, because it is impossible that the stage can represent exactly a house, or that the time of acting can be extended to twenty-four hours; therefore it is needless there should be any limitation whatever as to time or place, since otherwise it must be inferred, that there are degrees in impossibility, and that one thing may be more impossible than another.

The whole tone of the preface is that of one who wished to have it supposed, that he was writing concerning a subject rather beneath his notice, and only felt himself called forth to do so by the dogmatism of those who laid down confident rules or laws in matters so trifling. This affectation of supercilious censure appears deeply to have provoked Dryden, and prompted the acrimony of the following Defence, which he prefixed to a second edition of the Indian Emperor published in 1668, probably shortly after the offence had been given. The angry friends were afterwards reconciled; and Dryden, listening more to the feelings of former kindness than of recent passion, cancelled the Defence, which was never afterwards reprinted, till Congreve collected our author's dramatic works.

It is worthy of preservation, as it would be difficult to point out deeper contempt and irony, couched under language so temperate, cold, and outwardly respectful.

A DEFENCE OF AN ESSAY OF DRAMATIC POESY; BEING AN ANSWER TO THE PREFACE OF THE GREAT FAVOURITE, OR THE DUKE OF LERMA.

The former edition of "the Indian Emperor" being full of faults, which had escaped the printer, I have been willing to overlook this second with more care: and though I could not allow myself so much time as was necessary, yet by that little I have done, the press is freed from some errors which it had to answer for before. As for the more material faults of writing, which are properly mine, though I see many of them, I want leisure to amend them. It is enough for those who make one poem the business of their lives, to leave that correct: yet, excepting Virgil, I never met with any which was so in any language.

But while I was thus employed about this impression, there came to my hands a new printed play, called, "The Great Favourite, or, The Duke of Lerma;" the author of which, a noble and most ingenious person, has done me the favour to make some observations and animadversions upon my Dramatic Essay. I must confess he might have better consulted his reputation, than by matching himself with so weak an adversary. But if his honour be diminished in the choice of his antagonist, it is sufficiently recompensed in the election of his cause: which being the weaker, in all appearance, as combating the received opinions of the best ancient and modern authors, will add to his glory, if he overcome; and to the opinion of his generosity, if he be vanquished, since he engages at so great odds; and, so like a cavalier, undertakes the protection of the weaker party. I have only to fear, on my own behalf, that so good a cause as mine may not suffer by my ill management, or weak defence; yet I cannot in honour but take the glove when it is offered me; though I am only a champion by succession, and no more able to defend the right of Aristotle and Horace, than an infant Dimock[A] to maintain the title of a king.

[Footnote A: The family of Dimock, or Dymock, are hereditary champions of England; and, as such, obliged to maintain the king's title in single combat against all challengers.]

For my own concernment in the controversy, it is so small, that I can easily be contented to be driven from a few notions of dramatic poesy; especially by one, who has the reputation of understanding all things: and I might justly make that excuse for my yielding to him, which the philosopher made to the emperor; why should I offer to contend with him, who is master of more than twenty legions of arts and sciences? But I am forced to fight, and therefore it will be no shame to be overcome.

Yet I am so much his servant, as not to meddle with anything which does not concern me in his preface: therefore I leave the good sense and other excellencies of the first twenty lines, to be considered by the critics. As for the play of "The Duke of Lerma," having so much altered and beautified it as he has done, it can justly belong to none but him. Indeed they must be extremely ignorant, as well as envious, who would rob him of that honour; for you see him putting in his claim to it, even in the first two lines:

Repulse upon repulse, like waves thrown back,
That slide to hung upon obdurate rocks.

After this, let detraction do its worst; for if this be not his, it deserves to be. For my part, I declare for distributive justice; and from this, and what follows, he certainly deserves those advantages, which he acknowledges to have received from the opinion of sober men.

In the next place, I must beg leave to observe his great address in courting the reader to his party: For, intending to assault all poets, both ancient and modern, he discovers not his whole design at once, but seems only to aim at me, and attacks me on my weakest side, my defence of verse.

To begin with me, he gives me the compellation of "The Author of a Dramatic Essay;" which is a little discourse in dialogue, for the most part borrowed from the observations of others: therefore, that I may not be wanting to him in civility, I return his compliment, by calling him, "The Author of the Duke of Lerma."

But (that I may pass over his salute) he takes notice of my great pains to prove rhyme as natural in a serious play, and more effectual than blank verse. Thus indeed I did state the question; but he tells me, "I pursue that which I call natural in a wrong application; For 'tis not the question, whether rhyme, or not rhyme, be best, or most natural for a serious subject, but what is nearest the nature of that it represents."

If I have formerly mistaken the question, I must confess my ignorance so far, as to say I continue still in my mistake: But he ought to have proved that I mistook it; for it is yet but gratis dictum; I still shall think I have gained my point, if I can prove that rhyme is best, or most natural for a serious subject. As for the question as he states it, whether rhyme be nearest the nature of what it represents, I wonder he should think me so ridiculous as to dispute, whether prose or verse be nearest to ordinary conversation.

It still remains for him to prove his inference; that, since verse is granted to be more remote than prose from ordinary conversation, therefore no serious plays ought to be writ in verse: and when he clearly makes that good, I will acknowledge his victory as absolute as he can desire it.

The question now is, which of us two has mistaken it; and if it appear I have not, the world will suspect, "what gentleman that was, who was allowed to speak twice in parliament, because he had not yet spoken to the question[A];" and perhaps conclude it to be the same, who, as it is reported, maintained a contradiction in terminis, in the face of three hundred persons.

[Footnote A: A sneer which Sir Robert aims at Dryden. Dryden had written twice on the question of rhyming tragedies.]

But to return to verse, whether it be natural or not in plays, is a problem which is not demonstrable of either side: It is enough for me, that he acknowledges he had rather read good verse than prose: for if all the enemies of verse will confess as much, I shall not need to prove that it is natural. I am satisfied if it cause delight; for delight is the chief, if not the only, end of poesy: Instruction can be admitted but in the second place, for poesy only instructs as it delights. It is true, that to imitate well is a poet's work; but to affect the soul, and excite the passions, and, above all, to move admiration (which is the delight of serious plays), a bare imitation will not serve. The converse, therefore, which a poet is to imitate, must be heightened with all the arts and ornaments of poesy; and must be such as, strictly considered, could never be supposed spoken by any without premeditation.

As for what he urges, that "a play will still be supposed to be a composition of several persons speaking extempore, and that good verses are the hardest things which can be imagined to be so spoken;" I must crave leave to dissent from his opinion, as to the former part of it: For, if I am not somewhat in my behalf; for I say there, that this objection happens but seldom in a play; and then, too, either the meanness of the expression may be avoided, or shut out from the verse by breaking it in the midst.

But I have said too much in the defence of verse; for, after all, it is a very indifferent thing to me whether it obtain or not. I am content hereafter to be ordered by his rule, that is, to write it sometimes because it pleases me, and so much the rather, because he has declared that it pleases him. But he has taken his last farewell of the muses, and he has done it civilly, by honouring them with the name of "his long acquaintances," which is a compliment they have scarce deserved from him. For my own part, I bear a share in the public loss; and how emulous soever I may be of his fame and reputation, I cannot but give this testimony of his style, that it is extremely poetical, even in oratory; his thoughts elevated sometimes above common apprehension; his notions politic and grave, and tending to the instruction of princes, and reformation of states; that they are abundantly interlaced with variety of fancies, tropes, and figures, which the critics have enviously branded with the name of obscurity and false grammar.

"Well, he is now fettered in business of more unpleasant nature:" The muses have lost him, but the commonwealth gains by it; the corruption of a poet is the generation of a statesman.

"He will not venture again into the civil wars of censure, ubi—nullos habitura triumphos:" If he had not told us he had left the muses, we might have half suspected it by that word ubi, which does not any way belong to them in that place: the rest of the verse is indeed Lucan's, but that ubi, I will answer for it, is his own. Yet he has another reason for this disgust of poesy; for he says immediately after, that "the manner of plays which are now in most esteem is beyond his power to perform:" to perform the manner of a thing, I confess, is new English to me. "However, he condemns not the satisfaction of others, but rather their unnecessary understanding, who, like Sancho Panza's doctor, prescribe too strictly to our appetites; for," says he, "in the difference of tragedy and comedy, and of farce itself, there can be no determination but by the taste, nor in the manner of their composure."

We shall see him now as great a critic as he was a poet; and the reason why he excelled so much in poetry will be evident, for it will appear to have proceeded from the exactness of his judgment. "In the difference of tragedy, comedy, and farce itself, there can be no determination but by the taste." I will not quarrel with the obscurity of his phrase, though I justly might; but beg his pardon if I do not rightly understand him. If he means that there is no essential difference betwixt comedy, tragedy, and farce, but what is only made by the people's taste, which distinguishes one of them from the other, that is so manifest an error, that I need not lose time to contradict it. Were there neither judge, taste, nor opinion in the world, yet they would differ in their natures; for the action, character, and language of tragedy, would still be great and high; that of comedy, lower and more familiar. Admiration would be the delight of one, and satire of the other.

I have but briefly touched upon these things, because, whatever his words are, I can scarce imagine, that "he, who is always concerned for the true honour of reason, and would have no spurious issue fathered upon her," should mean any thing so absurd as to affirm, "that there is no difference betwixt comedy and tragedy but what is made by the taste only;" unless he would have us understand the comedies of my lord L. where the first act should be pottages, the second fricassees, &c. and the fifth a chere entiere of women.

I rather guess he means, that betwixt one comedy or tragedy and another, there is no other difference, but what is made by the liking or disliking of the audience. This is indeed a less error than the former, but yet it is a great one. The liking or disliking of the people gives the play the denomination of good or bad, but does not really make or constitute it such. To please the people ought to be the poet's aim, because plays are made for their delight; but it does not follow that they are always pleased with good plays, or that the plays which please them are always good. The humour of the people is now for comedy; therefore, in hope to please them, I write comedies rather than serious plays: and so far their taste prescribes to me. But it does not follow from that reason, that comedy is to be preferred before tragedy in its own nature; for that, which is so in its own nature, cannot be otherwise, as a man cannot but be a rational creature: But the opinion of the people may alter, and in another age, or perhaps in this, serious plays may be set up above comedies.

This I think a sufficient answer; if it be not, he has provided me of an excuse: it seems, in his wisdom, he foresaw my weakness, and has found out this expedient for me, "That it is not necessary for poets to study strict reason, since they are so used to a greater latitude than is allowed by that severe inquisition, that they must infringe their own jurisdiction, to profess themselves obliged to argue well."

I am obliged to him for discovering to me this back door; but I am not yet resolved on my retreat; for I am of opinion, that they cannot be good poets, who are not accustomed to argue well. False reasonings and colours of speech are the certain marks of one who does not understand the stage: for moral truth is the mistress of the poet as much as of the philosopher; poesy must resemble natural truth, but it must be ethical. Indeed, the poet dresses truth, and adorns nature, but does not alter them:

Ficta voluptatis causa sint proxima veris.

Therefore, that is not the best poesy, which resembles notions of things, that are not, to things that are: though the fancy may be great, and the words flowing, yet the soul is but half satisfied when there is not truth in the foundation. This is that which makes Virgil be preferred before the rest of poets. In variety of fancy, and sweetness of expression, you see Ovid far above him; for Virgil rejected many of those things which Ovid wrote. "A great wit's great work is to refuse," as my worthy friend Sir John Berkenhead has ingeniously expressed it: you rarely meet with any thing in Virgil but truth, which therefore leaves the strongest impression of pleasure in the soul. This I thought myself obliged to say in behalf of poesy; and to declare, though it be against myself, that when poets do not argue well, the defect is in the workmen, not in the art.

And now I come to the boldest part of his discourse, wherein he attacks not me, but all the ancients and moderns; and undermines, as he thinks, the very foundations on which Dramatic Poesy is built. I could wish he would have declined that envy which must of necessity follow such an undertaking, and contented himself with triumphing over me in my opinions of verse, which I will never hereafter dispute with him; but he must pardon me if I have that veneration for Aristotle, Horace, Ben Jonson, and Corneille, that I dare not serve him in such a cause, and against such heroes, but rather fight under their protection, as Homer reports of little Teucer, who shot the Trojans from under the large buckler of Ajax Telamon.

[Greek: Stae d ax up Aiantos sachei Telamoniadao]
He stood beneath his brother's ample shield;
And covered there, shot death through all the field.

The words of my noble adversary are these:

"But if we examine the general rules laid down for plays by strict reason, we shall find the errors equally gross; for the great foundation which is laid to build upon, is nothing as it is generally stated, as will appear upon the examination of the particulars."

These particulars in due time shall be examined. In the mean while, let us consider what this great foundation is, which he says is nothing, as it is generally stated. I never heard of any other foundation of Dramatic Poesy than the imitation of nature; neither was there ever pretended any other by the ancients or moderns, or me, who endeavour to follow them in that rule. This I have plainly said in my definition of a play; that it is a just and lively image of human nature, &c. Thus the foundation, as it is generally stated, will stand sure, if this definition of a play be true; if it be not, he ought to have made his exception against it, by proving that a play is not an imitation of nature, but somewhat else, which he is pleased to think it.

But 'tis very plain, that he has mistaken the foundation for that which is built upon it, though not immediately: for the direct and immediate consequence is this; if nature be to be imitated, then there is a rule for imitating nature rightly, otherwise there may be an end, and no means conducing to it. Hitherto I have proceeded by demonstration; but as our divines, when they have proved a Deity, because there is order, and have inferred that this Deity ought to be worshipped, differ afterwards in the manner of the worship; so, having laid down, that nature is to be imitated, and that proposition proving the next, that then there are means which conduce to the imitating of nature, I dare proceed no farther positively; but have only laid down some opinions of the ancients and moderns, and of my own, as means which they used, and which I thought probable for the attaining of that end. Those means are the same which my antagonist calls the foundations, how properly the world may judge; and to prove that this is his meaning, he clears it immediately to you, by enumerating those rules or propositions against which he makes his particular exceptions; as, namely, those of time and place, in these words: "First, we are told the plot should not be so ridiculously contrived, as to crowd two several countries into one stage; secondly, to cramp the accidents of many years or days into the representation of two hours and an half; and, lastly, a conclusion drawn, that the only remaining dispute is, concerning time, whether it should be contained in twelve or twenty-four hours; and the place to be limited to that spot of ground where the play is supposed to begin: and this is called nearest nature; for that is concluded most natural, which is most probable, and nearest to that which it presents."

Thus he has only made a small mistake, of the means conducing to the end for the end itself, and of the superstructure for the foundation: But he proceeds:

"To shew therefore upon what ill grounds they dictate laws for Dramatic Poesy," &c. He is here pleased to charge me with being magisterial, as he has done in many other places of his preface; therefore, in vindication of myself, I must crave leave to say, that my whole discourse was sceptical, according to that way of reasoning which was used by Socrates, Plato, and all the academics of old, which Tully and the best of the ancients followed, and which is imitated by the modest inquisitions of the Royal Society. That it is so, not only the name will shew, which is, An Essay, but the frame and composition of the work. You see it is a dialogue sustained by persons of several opinions, all of them left doubtful, to be determined by the readers in general; and more particularly deferred to the accurate judgment of my Lord Buckhurst, to whom I made a dedication of my book. These are my words in my epistle, speaking of the persons whom I introduced in my dialogue: "'Tis true they differed in their opinions, as 'tis probable they would: neither do I take upon me to reconcile, but to relate them, leaving your lordship to decide it in favour of that part which you shall judge most reasonable." And after that, in my advertisement to the reader, I said this: "The drift of the ensuing discourse is chiefly to vindicate the honour of our English writers from the censure of those who unjustly prefer the French before them. This I intimate, lest any should think me so exceeding vain, as to teach others an art, which they understand much better than myself." But this is more than necessary to clear my modesty in that point: and I am very confident, that there is scarce any man who has lost so much time, as to read that trifle, but will be my compurgator, as to that arrogance whereof I am accused. The truth is, if I had been naturally guilty of so much vanity as to dictate my opinions; yet I do not find that the character of a positive or self-conceited person is of such advantage to any in this age, that I should labour to be publicly admitted of that order.

But I am not now to defend my own cause, when that of all the ancients and moderns is in question. For this gentleman, who accuses me of arrogance, has taken a course not to be taxed with the other extreme of modesty. Those propositions, which are laid down in my discourse as helps to the better imitation of nature, are not mine (as I have said), nor were ever pretended so to be, but derived from the authority of Aristotle and Horace, and from the rules and examples of Ben Jonson and Corneille. These are the men with whom properly he contends, and against "whom he will endeavour to make it evident, that there is no such thing as what they all pretend."

His argument against the unities of place and time is this: "That 'tis as impossible for one stage to present two rooms or houses truly, as two countries or kingdoms; and as impossible that five hours or twenty-four hours should be two hours, as that a thousand hours or years should be less than what they are, or the greatest part of time to be comprehended in the less: for all of them being impossible, they are none of them nearest the truth, or nature of what they present; for impossibilities are all equal, and admit of no degree."

This argument is so scattered into parts, that it can scarce be united into a syllogism; yet, in obedience to him, I will abbreviate, and comprehend as much of it as I can in few words, that my answer to it may be more perspicuous. I conceive his meaning to be what follows, as to the unity of place: (if I mistake, I beg his pardon, professing it is not out of any design to play the Argumentative Poet.) If one stage cannot properly present two rooms or houses, much less two countries or kingdoms, then there can be no unity of place. But one stage cannot properly perform this: therefore there can be no unity of place.

I plainly deny his minor proposition; the force of which, if I mistake not, depends on this, that the stage being one place cannot be two. This indeed is as great a secret, as that we are all mortal; but to requite it with another, I must crave leave to tell him, that though the stage cannot be two places, yet it may properly represent them successively, or at several times. His argument is indeed no more than a mere fallacy, which will evidently appear when we distinguish place, as it relates to plays, into real and imaginary. The real place is that theatre, or piece of ground, on which the play is acted. The imaginary, that house, town, or country where the action of the drama is supposed to be, or, more plainly, where the scene of the play is laid. Let us now apply this to that Herculean argument, "which if strictly and duly weighed, is to make it evident, that there is no such thing as what they all pretend." 'Tis impossible, he says, for one stage to present two rooms or houses: I answer, 'tis neither impossible, nor improper, for one real place to represent two or more imaginary places, so it be done successively; which, in other words, is no more than this, that the imagination of the audience, aided by the words of the poet, and painted scenes, may suppose the stage to be sometimes one place, sometimes another; now a garden, or wood, and immediately a camp: which I appeal to every man's imagination, if it be not true. Neither the ancients nor moderns, as much fools as he is pleased to think them, ever asserted that they could make one place two; but they might hope, by the good leave of this author, that the change of a scene might lead the imagination to suppose the place altered: so that he cannot fasten those absurdities upon this scene of a play, or imaginary place of action, that it is one place, and yet two. And this being so clearly proved, that 'tis past any shew of a reasonable denial, it will not be hard to destroy that other part of his argument, which depends upon it, namely, that 'tis as impossible for a stage to represent two rooms or houses, as two countries or kingdoms: for his reason is already overthrown, which was, because both were alike impossible. This is manifestly otherwise; for 'tis proved that a stage may properly represent two rooms or houses; for the imagination being judge of what is represented, will in reason be less choked with the appearance of two rooms in the same house, or two houses in the same city, than with two distant cities in the same country, or two remote countries in the same universe. Imagination in a man, or reasonable creature, is supposed to participate of reason, and when that governs, as it does in the belief of fiction, reason is not destroyed, but misled, or blinded; that can prescribe to the reason, during the time of the representation, somewhat like a weak belief of what it sees and hears; and reason suffers itself to be so hood-winked, that it may better enjoy the pleasures of the fiction: But it is never so wholly made a captive, as to be drawn headlong into a persuasion of those things which are most remote from probability: It is in that case a free-born subject, not a slave; it will contribute willingly its assent, as far as it sees convenient, but will not be forced. Now, there is a greater vicinity in nature betwixt two rooms, than betwixt two houses; betwixt two houses, than betwixt two cities; and so of the rest: Reason, therefore, can sooner be led, by imagination, to step from one room into another, than to walk to two distant houses, and yet rather to go thither, than to fly like a witch through the air, and be hurried from one region to another. Fancy and Reason go hand in hand; the first cannot leave the last behind: And though Fancy, when it sees the wide gulph, would venture over, as the nimbler, yet it is with-held by Reason, which will refuse to take the leap, when the distance over it appears too large. If Ben Jonson himself will remove the scene from Rome into Tuscany in the same act, and from thence return to Rome, in the scene which immediately follows, reason will consider there is no proportionable allowance of time to perform the journey, and, therefore, will choose to stay at home. So, then, the less change of place there is, the less time is taken up in transporting the persons of the drama, with analogy to reason; and in that analogy, or resemblance of fiction to truth, consists the excellency of the play.

For what else concerns the unity of place, I have already given my opinion of it in my Essay, that there is a latitude to be allowed to it, as several places in the same town or city, or places adjacent to each other in the same country; which may all be comprehended under the larger denomination of one place; yet with this restriction, that the nearer and fewer those imaginary places are, the greater resemblance they will have to truth; and reason, which cannot make them one, will be more easily led to suppose them so.

What has been said of the unity of place, may easily be applied to that of time: I grant it to be impossible, that the greater part of time should be comprehended in the less, that twenty-four hours should be crowded into three: But there is no necessity of that supposition; for as place, so time relating to a play, is either imaginary or real: The real is comprehended in those three hours, more or less, in the space of which the play is represented; the imaginary is that which is supposed to be taken up in the representation, as twenty-four hours, more or less. Now, no man ever could suppose, that twenty-four real hours could be included in the space of three; but where is the absurdity of affirming, that the feigned business of twenty-four imagined hours, may not more naturally be represented in the compass of three real hours, than the like feigned business of twenty-four years, in the same proportion of real time? For the proportions are always real, and much nearer, by his permission, of twenty-four to three, than of four thousand to it.

I am almost fearful of illustrating any thing by similitude, lest he should confute it for an argument; yet I think the comparison of a glass will discover very aptly the fallacy of his argument, both concerning time and place. The strength of his reason depends on this, that the less cannot comprehend the greater. I have already answered, that we need not suppose it does; I say not that the less can comprehend the greater, but only, that it may represent it. As in a glass, or mirror, of half-a-yard diameter, a whole room, and many persons in it, may be seen at once; not that it can comprehend that room, or those persons, but that it represents them to the sight.

But the author of the "Duke of Lerma" is to be excused for his declaring against the unity of time; for, if I be not much mistaken, he is an interested person;—the time of that play taking up so many years, as the favour of the Duke of Lerma continued; nay, the second and third act including all the time of his prosperity, which was a great part of the reign of Philip the Third: For in the beginning of the second act he was not yet a favourite, and, before the end of the third, was in disgrace. I say not this with the least design of limiting the stage too servilely to twenty-four hours, however he be pleased to tax me with dogmatising on that point, In my dialogue, as I before hinted, several persons maintained their several opinions: One of them, indeed, who supported the cause of the French poesy, said how strict they were in that particular; but he who answered, in behalf of our nation, was willing to give more latitude to the rule, and cites the words of Corneille himself, complaining against the severity of it, and observing, what beauties it banished from the stage, p. 44. of my Essay. In few words, my own opinion is this, (and I willingly submit it to my adversary, when he will please impartially to consider it) that the imaginary time of every play ought to be contrived into as narrow a compass, as the nature of the plot, the quality of the persons, and variety of accidents will allow. In comedy, I would not exceed twenty-four or thirty hours; for the plot, accidents, and persons, of comedy are small, and may be naturally turned in a little compass: But in tragedy, the design is weighty, and the persons great; therefore, there will naturally be required a greater space of time in which to move them. And this, though Ben Jonson has not told us, yet it is manifestly his opinion: For you see that to his comedies he allows generally but twenty-four hours; to his two tragedies, "Sejanus," and "Catiline," a much larger time, though he draws both of them into as narrow a compass as he can: For he shews you only the latter end of Sejanus's favour, and the conspiracy of Catiline already ripe, and just breaking out into action.

But as it is an error, on the one side, to make too great a disproportion betwixt the imaginary time of the play, and the real time of its representation; so, on the other side, it is an oversight to compress the accidents of a play into a narrower compass than that in which they could naturally be produced. Of this last error the French are seldom guilty, because the thinness of their plots prevents them from it; but few Englishmen, except Ben Jonson, have ever made a plot, with variety of design in it, included in twenty-four hours, which was altogether natural. For this reason, I prefer the "Silent Woman" before all other plays, I think justly, as I do its author, in judgment, above all other poets. Yet, of the two, I think that error the most pardonable, which in too strait a compass crowds together many accidents, since it produces more variety, and, consequently, more pleasure to the audience; and, because the nearness of proportion betwixt the imaginary and real time, does speciously cover the compression of the accidents.

Thus I have endeavoured to answer the meaning of his argument; for, as he drew it, I humbly conceive that it was none,—as will appear by his proposition, and the proof of it. His proposition was this:

"If strictly and duly weighed, it is as impossible for one stage to present two rooms, or houses, as two countries, or kingdoms," &c. And his proof this: "For all being impossible, they are none of them nearest the truth or nature of what they present."

Here you see, instead of proof or reason, there is only petitio principii. For, in plain words, his sense is this: Two things are as impossible as one another, because they are both equally impossible: But he takes those two things to be granted as impossible, which he ought to have proved such, before he had proceeded to prove them equally impossible: He should have made out first, that it was impossible for one stage to represent two houses, and then have gone forward to prove, that it was as equally impossible for a stage to present two houses, as two countries.

After all this, the very absurdity, to which he would reduce me, is none at all: For he only drives at this, that, if his argument be true, I must then acknowledge that there are degrees in impossibilities, which I easily grant him without dispute; and, if I mistake not, Aristotle and the School are of my opinion. For there are some things which are absolutely impossible, and others which are only so ex parte; as it is absolutely impossible for a thing to be, and not to be at the same time: But for a stone to move naturally upward, is only impossible ex parte materiae; but it is not impossible for the first mover to alter the nature of it.

His last assault, like that of a Frenchman, is most feeble; for whereas I have observed, that none have been violent against verse, but such only as have not attempted it, or have succeeded ill in their attempt, he will needs, according to his usual custom, improve my observation to an argument, that he might have the glory to confute it, But I lay my observation at his feet, as I do my pen, which I have often employed willingly in his deserved commendations, and now most unwillingly against his judgment. For his person and parts, I honour them as much as any man living, and have had so many particular obligations to him, that I should be very ungrateful, if I did not acknowledge them to the world. But I gave not the first occasion of this difference in opinions. In my epistle dedicatory, before my "Rival Ladies," I had said somewhat in behalf of verse, which he was pleased to answer in his preface to his plays. That occasioned my reply in my essay; and that reply begot this rejoinder of his, in his preface to the "Duke of Lerna." But as I was the last who took up arms, I will be the first to lay them down. For what I have here written, I submit it wholly to him; and if I do not hereafter answer what may be objected against this paper, I hope the world will not impute it to any other reason, than only the due respect which I have for so noble an opponent.

THE INDIAN EMPEROR

The Indian Emperor is the first of Dryden's plays which exhibited, in a marked degree, the peculiarity of his stile, and drew upon him the attention of the world. Without equalling the extravagancies of the Conquest of Granada, and the Royal Martyr, works produced when our author was emboldened, by public applause, to give full scope to his daring genius, the following may be considered as a model of the heroic drama, A few words, therefore, will not be here misplaced, on the nature of the kind of tragedies, in which, during the earlier part of his literary career, our author delighted and excelled.

The heroic, or rhyming, plays, were borrowed from the French, to whose genius they are better suited than to the British. An analogy may be observed between all the different departments of the belles lettres; and none seem more closely allied, than the pursuits of the dramatic writer, and those of the composer of romances or novels. Both deal in fictitious adventure; both write for amusement; and address themselves nearly to the same class of admirers. Nay, although the pride of the dramatist may be offended by the assertion, it would seem, that the nature of his walk is often prescribed by the successful impression of a novel upon the public mind. If we laugh over low adventures in a novel, we soon see low comedy upon the stage: If we are horror-struck with a tale of robbers and murder in our closet, the dagger and the green carpet will not long remain unemployed in the theatre; and if ghosts haunt our novels, they soon stalk amongst our scenes. Under this persuasion, we have little doubt that the heroic tragedies were the legitimate offspring of the French romances of Calprenede and Scuderi. Such as may deign to open these venerable and neglected tomes, will be soon convinced of their extreme resemblance to the heroic drama. A remarkable feature in both, is the ideal world which they form for themselves. Every sentiment is lofty, splendid, and striking; and no apology is admitted for any departure from the dignity of character, however natural or impressive. The beauty of the heroine, and the valour of the hero, must be alike resistless; and the moving spring, through the whole action, is the overbearing passion of love. Their language and manners are as peculiar to themselves, as their prowess and susceptibility. The pastoral Arcadian does not differ more widely from an ordinary rustic, than these lofty persons do from the princes and kings of this world. Neither is any circumstance of national character, or manners, allowed as an apology for altering the established character, which must be invariably sustained by the persons of the heroic drama. The religion, and the state of society of the country where the scene is laid, may be occasionally alluded to as authority for varying a procession, or introducing new dresses and decorations; but, in all other respects, an Indian Inca, attired in feathers, must hold the same dignity of deportment, and display the same powers of declamation, and ingenuity of argument, with a Roman emperor in his purple, or a feudal warrior in his armour; for the rule and decorum of this species of composition is too peremptory, to give way either to the current of human passions, or to the usages of nations. Gibbon has remarked, that the kings of the Gepidae, and the Ostrogoths in Corneille's tragedy of Attila, are profound politicians, and sentimental lovers;—a description which, with a varying portion of pride, courtesy, and heroism, will apply to almost all the characters in plays drawn upon this model.

It is impossible to conceive anything more different from the old English drama, than the heroic plays which were introduced by Charles II. The former, in labouring to exhibit a variety and contrast of passions, tempers, or humours, frequently altogether neglected the dignity of the scene. In the heroical tragedy, on the other hand, nothing was to be indecorous, nothing grotesque: The personages were to speak, not as men, but as heroes; to whom, as statuaries have assigned a superiority of stature, so these poets have given an uniform grandeur of feeling and of expression. It may be thought, that this monotonous splendour of diction would have palled upon an English audience, less pleased generally with refinement, however elegant, than with bursts of passion, and flights of novelty. But Dryden felt his force in the line which he chose to pursue and recommend. The indescribable charms of his versification gratified the ear of the public, while their attention was engaged by the splendour of his images, and the matchless ingenuity of his arguments. It must also be admitted, that, by their total neglect of the unities, our ancient dramatic authors shocked the feelings of the more learned, and embarrassed the understanding of the less acute, among the spectators. We do not hold it treason to depart from the strict rules respecting time and place, inculcated by the ancients, and followed in the heroic plays. But it will surely be granted to us, that, where they can be observed, without the sacrifice of great beauties, or incurring such absurdities as Dennis has justly charged upon Cato, the play will be proportionally more intelligible on the stage, and more pleasing in the closet. And although we willingly censure the practice of driving argument, upon the stage, into metaphysical refinement, and rendering the contest of contrasted passions a mere combat in logic, yet we must equally condemn those tragedies, in which the poet sketches out the character with a few broken common-places, expressive of love, of rage, or of grief, and leaves the canvas to be filled up by the actor, according to his own taste, power, and inclination.

The Indian Emperor is an instance, what beautiful poetry may be united to, we had almost said thrown away upon, the heroic drama. The very first scene exhibits much of those beauties, and their attendant deformities. A modern audience would hardly have sate in patience to hear more than the first extravagant and ludicrous supposition of Cortez:

As if our old world modestly withdrew;
And here, in private, had brought forth a new.

But had they condemned the piece for this uncommon case of parturition, they would have lost the beautiful and melodious verses, in which Cortez, and his followers, describe the advantages of the newly discovered world; and they would have lost the still more exquisite account, which, immediately after, Guyomar gives of the arrival of the Spanish fleet. Of the characters little need be said; they stalk on, in their own fairy land, in the same uniform livery, and with little peculiarity of discrimination. All the men, from Montezuma down to Pizarro, are brave warriors; and only vary, in proportion to the mitigating qualities which the poet has infused into their military ardour. The women are all beautiful, and all deeply in love; differing from each other only, as the haughty or tender predominates in their passion. But the charm of the poetry, and the ingenuity of the dialogue, render it impossible to peruse, without pleasure, a drama, the faults of which may be imputed to its structure, while its beauties are peculiar to Dryden.

The plot of the Indian Emperor is certainly of our author's own composition; since even the malignant assiduity of Langbaine has been unable to point out any author from whom it is borrowed. The play was first acted in 1665, and received with great applause.

CONNECTION OF THE INDIAN EMPEROR TO THE INDIAN QUEEN [A]

[Footnote A: This argument was printed, and dispersed amongst the audience upon the first night of representation. Hence Bayes is made to say, in the Rehearsal, that he had printed many reams, to instil into the audience some conception of his plot.]

The conclusion of the Indian Queen (part of which poem was wrote by me) left little matter for another story to be built on, there remaining but two of the considerable characters alive, viz. Montezuma and Orazia. Thereupon the author of this thought it necessary to produce new persons from the old ones; and considering the late Indian Queen, before she loved Montezuma, lived in clandestine marriage with her general Traxalla, from those two he has raised a son and two daughters, supposed to be left young orphans at their death. On the other side, he has given to Montezuma and Orazia, two sons and a daughter; all now supposed to be grown up to mens' and womens' estate; and their mother, Orazia, (for whom there was no further use in the story,) lately dead.

So that you are to imagine about twenty years elapsed since the coronation of Montezuma; who, in the truth of the history, was a great and glorious prince; and in whose time happened the discovery and invasion of Mexico, by the Spaniards, under the conduct of Hernando Cortez, who, joining with the Traxallan Indians, the inveterate enemies of Montezuma, wholly subverted that flourishing empire; the conquest of which is the subject of this dramatic poem.

I have neither wholly followed the story, nor varied from it; and, as near as I could, have traced the native simplicity and ignorance of the Indians, in relation to European customs;—the shipping, armour, horses, swords, and guns of the Spaniards, being as new to them, as their habits and their language were to the Christians.

The difference of their religion from ours, I have taken from the story itself; and that which you find of it in the first and fifth acts, touching the sufferings and constancy of Montezuma in his opinions, I have only illustrated, not altered, from those who have written of it.

PROLOGUE
Almighty critics! whom our Indians here
Worship, just as they do the devil—for fear;

In reverence to your power, I come this day,
To give you timely warning of our play.
The scenes are old, the habits are the same
We wore last year, before the Spaniards came[A].
Now, if you stay, the blood, that shall be shed
From this poor play, be all upon your head.
We neither promise you one dance, or show;
Then plot, and language, they are wanting too:
But you, kind wits, will those light faults excuse,
Those are the common frailties of the muse;
Which, who observes, he buys his place too dear;
For 'tis your business to be cozened here.
These wretched spies of wit must then confess,
They take more pains to please themselves the less.
Grant us such judges, Phoebus, we request,
As still mistake themselves into a jest;
Such easy judges, that our poet may
Himself admire the fortune of his play;
And, arrogantly, as his fellows do,
Think he writes well, because he pleases you.
This he conceives not hard to bring about,
If all of you would join to help him out:
Would each man take but what he understands,
And leave the rest upon the poet's hands.

[Footnote A: Alluding to the Indian Queen, in which the scene is laid before the arrival of the Spaniards in America, and which was acted in 1664, as this was in 1665.]

DRAMATIS PERSONAE

INDIAN MEN
MONTEZUMA, Emperor of Mexico.
ODMAR, his eldest son.
GUYOMAR, his younger son.
ORBELLAN, son of the late Indian Queen by TRAXALLA.
High Priest of the Sun.

WOMEN
CYDARIA, MONTEZUMA'S daughter.
ALMERIA, Sisters; and daughters to the late
ALIBECH, Indian Queen.

SPANIARDS.
CORTEZ, the Spanish General.
VASQUEZ, Commanders under him.
PIZARRO,

SCENE—Mexico, and two leagues about it.

ACT I

SCENE I —A pleasant Indian country

Enter Cortez, Vasquez, Pizarro, with Spaniards and Indians of their party.

CORTEZ - On what new happy climate are we thrown,
So long kept secret, and so lately known;
As if our old world modestly withdrew,
And here in private had brought forth a new?

VASQUEZ - Corn, oil, and wine, are wanting to this ground,
In which our countries fruitfully abound;
As if this infant world, yet unarrayed,
Naked and bare in Nature's lap were laid.
No useful arts have yet found footing here,
But all untaught and savage does appear.

CORTEZ - Wild and untaught are terms which we alone
Invent, for fashions differing from our own;
For all their customs are by nature wrought,
But we, by art, unteach what nature taught.

PIZARRO - In Spain, our springs, like old men's children, be
Decayed and withered from their infancy:
No kindly showers fall on our barren earth,
To hatch the season in a timely birth:
Our summer such a russet livery wears,
As in a garment often dyed appears.

CORTEZ - Here nature spreads her fruitful sweetness round,
Breathes on the air, and broods upon the ground:
Here days and nights the only seasons be;
The sun no climate does so gladly see:
When forced from hence, to view our parts, he mourns;
Takes little journies, and makes quick returns.

VASQUEZ - Methinks, we walk in dreams on Fairy-land,
Where golden ore lies mixt with common sand;
Each downfal of a flood, the mountains pour
From their rich bowels, rolls a silver shower.
Heaven from all ages wisely did provide
This wealth, and for the bravest nation hide,
Who, with four hundred foot and forty horse,
Dare boldly go a new-found world to force.

PIZARRO - Our men, though valiant, we should find too few,
But Indians join the Indians to subdue;
Taxallan, shook by Montezuma's powers,
Has, to resist his forces, called in ours.

VASQUEZ - Rashly to arm against so great a king,
I hold not safe; nor is it just to bring
A war, without a fair defiance made.

PIZARRO - Declare we first our quarrel; then invade.

CORTEZ - Myself, my king's ambassador, will go;
Speak, Indian guide, how far to Mexico?

Ind. Your eyes can scarce so far a prospect make,
As to discern the city on the lake;
But that broad causeway will direct your way,
And you may reach the town by noon of day.

CORTEZ - Command a party of our Indians out,
With a strict charge, not to engage, but scout:
By noble ways we conquest will prepare;
First, offer peace, and, that refused, make war.

[Exeunt.

SCENE II—A Temple

The High Priest with other Priests. To them an Indian.

INDIAN - Haste, holy priest, it is the king's command.

HIGH PRIEST - When sets he forward?

INDIAN - He is near at hand.

HIGH PRIEST - The incense is upon the altar placed,
The bloody sacrifice already past;
Five hundred captives saw the rising sun,
Who lost their light, ere half his race was run.
That which remains we here must celebrate;
Where, far from noise, without the city gate,
The peaceful power that governs love repairs,
To feast upon soft vows and silent prayers.
We for his royal presence only stay,
To end the rites of this so solemn day.
[Exit Indian.

Enter Montezuma; his eldest son, Odmar; his daughter, Cydaria; Almeria, Alibech, Orbellan, and
Train. They place themselves.

HIGH PRIEST - On your birthday, while we sing
To our gods and to our king,
Her, among this beauteous quire,
Whose perfections you admire,
Her, who fairest does appear,
Crown her queen of all the year,
Of the year and of the day,
And at her feet your garland lay.
ODMAR - My father this way does his looks direct;
Heaven grant, he give it not where I suspect!

[Montezuma rises, goes about the Ladies, and at length stays at Almeria, and bows.

MONTEZUMA - Since my Orazia's death, I have not seen
A beauty, so deserving to be queen
As fair Almeria.

ALMERIA - Sure he will not know

[To her brother and sister, aside.

My birth I to that injured princess owe,
Whom his hard heart not only love denied,
But in her sufferings took unmanly pride.

ALIBECH - Since Montezuma will his choice renew,
In dead Orazia's room electing you,
'Twill please our mother's ghost that you succeed
To all the glories of her rival's bed.

ALMERIA - If news be carried to the shades below,
The Indian queen will be more pleased, to know,
That I his scorns on him, who scorned her, pay.

ORBELLAN - Would you could right her some more noble way!

[She turns to him, who is kneeling all this while.

MONTEZUMA - Madam, this posture is for heaven designed,

[Kneeling.

And what moves heaven I hope may make you kind.

ALMERIA - Heaven may be kind; the gods uninjured live.
And crimes below cost little to forgive:
By thee, inhuman, both my parents died;
One by thy sword, the other by thy pride.

MONTEZUMA - My haughty mind no fate could ever bow,

Yet I must stoop to one, who scorns me now:
Is there no pity to my sufferings due?

ALMERIA - As much as what my mother found from you.

MONTEZUMA - Your mother's wrongs a recompence shall meet;
I lay my sceptre at her daughter's feet.

ALMERIA - He, who does now my least commands obey,
Would call me queen, and take my power away.

ODMAR - Can he hear this, and not his fetters break?
Is love so powerful, or his soul so weak?
I'll fright her from it.—Madam, though you see
The king is kind, I hope your modesty
Will know, what distance to the crown is due.

ALMERIA - Distance and modesty prescribed by you!

ODMAR - Almeria dares not think such thoughts as these.

ALMERIA - She dares both think and act what thoughts she please.
Tis much below me on his throne to sit;
But when I do, you shall petition it.

ODMAR - If, sir, Almeria does your bed partake,
I mourn for my forgotten mother's' sake.

MONTEZUMA - When parents' loves are ordered by a son,
Let streams prescribe their fountains where to run.

ODMAR - In all I urge, I keep my duty still,
Not rule your reason, but instruct your will.

MONTEZUMA - Small use of reason in that prince is shown,
Who follows others, and neglects his own.

[Almeria to Orbellan and Alibech, who are this while whispering to her.

ALMERIA - No, he shall ever love, and always be
The subject of my scorn and cruelty.

ORBELLAN - To prove the lasting torment of his life,
You must not be his mistress, but his wife.
Few know what care an husband's peace destroys,
His real griefs, and his dissembled joys.

ALMERIA - What mark of pleasing vengeance could be shown,
If I, to break his quiet, lose my own?

ORBELLAN - A brother's life upon your love relics,

Since I do homage to Cydaria's eyes:
How can her father to my hopes be kind,
If in your heart he no example find?

ALMERIA - To save your life I'll suffer any thing,
Yet I'll not flatter this tempestuous king;
But work his stubborn soul a nobler way,
And, if he love, I'll force him to obey.
I take this garland, not as given by you,

[To Montezuma

But as my merit and my beauty's due.
As for the crown, that you, my slave, possess,
To share it with you would but make me less.

Enter Guyomar hastily.

ODMAR - My brother Guyomar! methinks I spy
Haste in his steps, and wonder in his eye.

MONTEZUMA - I sent thee to the frontiers; quickly tell
The cause of thy return; are all things well?

GUYOMAR - I went, in order, sir, to your command,
To view the utmost limits of the land:
To that sea-shore where no more world is found,
But foaming billows breaking on the ground;
Where, for a while, my eyes no object met,
But distant skies, that in the ocean set;
And low-hung clouds, that dipt themselves in rain,
To shake their fleeces on the earth again.
At last, as far as I could cast my eyes
Upon the sea, somewhat, methought, did rise,
Like blueish mists, which, still appearing more,
Took dreadful shapes, and moved towards the shore.

MONTEZUMA - What forms did these new wonders represent?

GUYOMAR - More strange than what your wonder can invent.
The object, I could first distinctly view,
Was tall straight trees, which on the waters flew;
Wings on their sides, instead of leaves, did grow,
Which gathered all the breath the winds could blow:
And at their roots grew floating palaces,
Whose outblowed bellies cut the yielding seas.

MONTEZUMA - What divine monsters, O ye gods, were these,
That float in air, and fly upon the seas!
Came they alive, or dead, upon the shore?

GUYOMAR - Alas, they lived too sure; I heard them roar.
All turned their sides, and to each other spoke;
I saw their words break out in fire and smoke.
Sure 'tis their voice, that thunders from on high,
Or these the younger brothers of the sky.
Deaf with the noise, I took my hasty flight;
No mortal courage can support the fright.

HIGH PRIEST - Old prophecies foretel our fall at hand,
When bearded men in floating castles land.
I fear it is of dire portent.

MONTEZUMA - Go see
What it foreshows, and what the gods decree.
Meantime proceed we to what rites remain.
Odmar, of all this presence does contain,
Give her your wreath, whom you esteem most fair.

ODMAR - Above the rest I judge one beauty rare,
And may that beauty prove as kind to me,
[He gives ALIBECH the wreath.
As I am sure fair Alibech is she.

MONTEZUMA - You, Guyomar, must next perform your part.

GUYOMAR - I want a garland, but I'll give a heart:
My brother's pardon I must first implore,
Since I with him fair Alibech adore.

ODMAR - That all should Alibech adore, 'tis true;
But some respect is to my birthright due.
My claim to her by eldership I prove.

GUYOMAR - Age is a plea in empire, not in love.

ODMAR - I long have staid for this solemnity,
To make my passion public.

GUYOMAR - So have I.

ODMAR - But from her birth my soul has been her slave;
My heart received the first wounds which she save:
I watched the early glories of her eyes,
As men for daybreak watch the eastern skies.

GUYOMAR - It seems my soul then moved the quicker pace;
Yours first set out, mine reached her in the race.

MONTEZUMA - Odmar, your choice I cannot disapprove;
Nor justly, Guyomar, can blame your love.
To Alibech alone refer your suit,

And let her sentence finish your dispute.

ALIBECH - You think me, sir, a mistress quickly won.
So soon to finish what is scarce begun:
In this surprise should I a judgment make,
'Tis answering riddles ere I'm well awake:
If you oblige me suddenly to chuse,
The choice is made, for I must both refuse:
For to myself I owe this due regard,
Not to make love my gift, but my reward.
Time best will show, whose services will last.

ODMAR - Then judge my future service by my past.
What I shall be, by what I was, you know:
That love took deepest root, which first did grow.

GUYOMAR - That love, which first was set, will first decay;
Mine, of a fresher date, will longer stay.

ODMAR - Still you forget my birth.

GUYOMAR - But you, I see,
Take care still to refresh my memory.

MONTEZUMA - My sons, let your unseemly discord cease,
If not in friendship, live at least in peace.
Orbellan, where you love, bestow your wreath.

ORBELLAN - My love I dare not, even in whispers, breathe.

MONTEZUMA - A virtuous love may venture any thing.

ORBELLAN - Not to attempt the daughter of my king.

MONTEZUMA - Whither is all my former fury gone?
Once more I have Traxalla's chains put on,
And by his children am in triumph led:
Too well the living have revenged the dead!

ALMERIA - You think my brother born your enemy;
He's of Traxalla's blood, and so am I.

MONTEZUMA - In vain I strive.
My lion-heart is with love's toils beset;
Struggling I fall still deeper in the net.
Cydaria, your new lover's garland take,
And use him kindly for your father's sake.

CYDARIA - So strong an hatred does my nature sway.
That, spite of duty, I must disobey:
Besides, you warned me still of loving two;

Can I love him, already loving you?
Enter a Guard hastily.

MONTEZUMA - You look amazed, as if some sudden fear
Had seized your hearts; is any danger near?

FIRST GUARD - Behind the covert, where this temple stands,
Thick as the shades, there issue swarming bands
Of ambushed men, whom, by their arms and dress,
To be Taxallan enemies I guess.

SECOND GUARD - The temple, sir, is almost compassed round.

MONTEZUMA - Some speedy way for passage must be found.
Make to the city by the postern gate,
I'll either force my victory, or fate;
A glorious death in arms I'll rather prove,
Than stay to perish tamely by my love.

[Exeunt.

An alarm within. Enter Montezuma, Odmar, Guyomar, Alibech, Orbellan, Cydaria, Almeria, as
pursued by Taxallans.

MONTEZUMA - No succour from the town?

ODMAR - None, none is nigh.

GUYOMAR - We are inclosed, and must resolve to die.

MONTEZUMA - Fight for revenge, now hope of life is past
But one stroke more, and that will be my last.

Enter Cortez, Vasquez, Pizarro, to the Taxallans: Cortez stays them, just falling on.

CORTEZ - Contemned? my orders broke even in my sight?
Did I not strictly charge, you should not fight?

[To his Indians.

INDIAN - Your choler, general, does unjustly rise,
To see your friends pursue your enemies.
The greatest and most cruel foes we have,
Are these, whom you would ignorantly save.
By ambushed men, behind their temple laid,
We have the king of Mexico betrayed.

CORTEZ - Where, banished virtue, wilt thou shew thy face,
If treachery infects thy Indian race?
Dismiss your rage, and lay your weapons by:
Know I protect them, and they shall not die.

INDIAN - O wondrous mercy, shewn to foes distrest!

CORTEZ - Call them not so, when once with odds opprest;
Nor are they foes my clemency defends,
Until they have refused the name of friends:
Draw up our Spaniards by themselves, then fire
Our guns on all, who do not strait retire.

[To Vasquez

Indian, O mercy, mercy! at thy feet we fall,

[Indians kneeling.

Before thy roaring Gods destroy us all:
See, we retreat without the least reply;
Keep thy Gods silent! if they speak we die.

[The Taxallans retire.

MONTEZUMA - The fierce Taxatlans lay their weapons down,
Some miracle in our relief is shewn.

GUYOMAR - These bearded men in shape and colour be
Like those I saw come floating on the sea.

[Montezuma kneels to Cortez

MONTEZUMA - Patron of Mexico, and God of wars,
Son of the sun, and brother of the stars—

CORTEZ - Great monarch, your devotion you misplace.

MONTEZUMA - Thy actions shew thee born of heavenly race.
If then thou art that cruel God, whose eyes
Delight in blood, and human sacrifice,
Thy dreadful altars I with slaves will store,
And feed thy nostrils with hot reeking gore;
Or if that mild and gentle God thou be,
Who dost mankind below with pity see,
With breath of incense I will glad thy heart;
But if, like us, of mortal seed thou art,
Presents of choicest fowls, and fruits I'll bring,
And in my realms thou shalt be more than king.

CORTEZ - Monarch of empires, and deserving more
Than the sun sees upon your western shore;
Like you a man, and hither led by fame,
Not by constraint, but by my choice, I came;
Ambassador of peace, if peace you chuse,

Or herald of a war, if you refuse.

MONTEZUMA - Whence, or from whom, dost thou these offers bring?

CORTEZ - From Charles the Fifth, the world's most potent king.

MONTEZUMA - Some petty prince, and one of little fame,
For to this hour I never heard his name:
The two great empires of the world I know,
That of Peru, and this of Mexico;
And since the earth none larger does afford,
This Charles is some poor tributary lord.

CORTEZ - You speak of that small part of earth you know;
But betwixt us and you wide oceans flow,
And watry desarts of so vast extent,
That passing hither four full moons we spent.

MONTEZUMA - But say, what news, what offers dost thou bring
From so remote, and so unknown a king?

[While Vasquez speaks, Cortez spies the ladies and goes to them, entertaining Cydaria with courtship in dumb shew.

VASQUEZ - Spain's mighty monarch, to whom heaven thinks fit,
That all the nations of the earth submit,
In gracious clemency, does condescend
On these conditions to become your friend.
First, that of him you shall your sceptre hold;
Next, you present him with your useless gold:
Last, that you leave those idols you implore,
And one true deity with him adore.

MONTEZUMA - You speak your prince a mighty emperor,
But his demands have spoke him proud and poor;
He proudly at my free-born sceptre flies,
Yet poorly begs a metal I despise.
Gold thou mayest take, whatever thou canst find,
Save what for sacred uses is designed:
But, by what right pretends your king to be
The sovereign lord of all the world and me?

PIZARRO - The sovereign priest—
Who represents on earth the power of heaven,
Has this your empire to our monarch given.

MONTEZUMA - Ill does he represent the powers above,
Who nourishes debate, not preaches love;
Besides, what greater folly can be shewn?
He gives another what is not his own.

VASQUEZ - His power must needs unquestioned be below,
For he in heaven an empire can bestow.

MONTEZUMA - Empires in heaven he with more ease may give,
And you, perhaps, would with less thanks receive;
But heaven has need of no such viceroy here,
Itself bestows the crowns that monarchs wear.

PIZARRO - You wrong his power, as you mistake our end,
Who came thus far religion to extend.

MONTEZUMA - He, who religion truly understands,
Knows its extent must be in men, not lands.

ODMAR - But who are those that truth must propagate
Within the confines of my father's state?

VASQUEZ - Religious men, who hither must be sent
As awful guides of heavenly government;
To teach you penance, fasts, and abstinence,
To punish bodies for the soul's offence.

MONTEZUMA - Cheaply you sin, and punish crimes with ease,
Not as the offended, but the offenders please;
First injure heaven, and, when its wrath is due,
Yourselves prescribe it how to punish you.

ODMAR - What numbers of these holy men must come?

PIZARRO - You shall not want, each village shall have some;
Who, though the royal dignity they own,
Are equal to it, and depend on none.

GUYOMAR - Depend on none! you treat them sure in state,
For 'tis their plenty does their pride create.

MONTEZUMA - Those ghostly kings would parcel out my power,
And all the fatness of my land devour.
That monarch sits not safely on his throne
Who bears, within, a power that shocks his own.
They teach obedience to imperial sway,
But think it sin if they themselves obey.

VASQUEZ - It seems, then, our religion you accuse,
And peaceful homage to our king refuse.

MONTEZUMA - Your Gods I slight not, but will keep my own;
My crown is absolute, and holds of none.
I cannot in a base subjection live,
Nor suffer you to take, though I would give.

CORTEZ - Is this your answer, sir?

MONTEZUMA - This, as a prince,
Bound to my people's and my crown's defence,
I must return; but, as a man, by you
Redeemed from death, all gratitude is due.

CORTEZ - It was an act my honour bound me to:
But what I did, were I again to do,
I could not do it on my honour's score,
For love would now oblige me to do more.
Is no way left that we may yet agree?
Must I have war, yet have no enemy?

VASQUEZ - He has refused all terms of peace to take.

MONTEZUMA - Since we must fight, hear, heavens, what prayers I make!
First, to preserve this ancient state and me,
But if your doom the fall of both decree,
Grant only he, who has such honour shewn,
When I am dust, may fill my empty throne!

CORTEZ - To make me happier than that wish can do,
Lies not in all your Gods to grant, but you;
Let this fair princess but one minute stay,
A look from her will your obligements pay.

[Exeunt Montezuma, Odmar, Guyomar, Orbellan, Almeria, and Alibech.

MONTEZUMA [to Cydaria] - Your duty in your quick return be shewn.
Stay you, and wait my daughter to the town.

[To his guards.

[Cydaria is going, but turns and looks back upon Cortez, who is looking on her all this while.

CYDARIA - My father's gone, and yet I cannot go;
Sure I have something lost or left behind!

[Aside.

CORTEZ - Like travellers who wander in the snow,
I on her beauty gaze 'till I am blind.

[Aside.

CYDARIA - Thick breath, quick pulse, and heaving of my heart,
All signs of some unwonted change appear:
I find myself unwilling to depart,
And yet I know not why I would be here.
Stranger, you raise such torments in my breast,

That when I go, (if I must go again)
I'll tell my father you have robbed my rest,
And to him of your injuries complain.

CORTEZ - Unknown, I swear, those wrongs were which I wrought,
But my complaints will much more just appear,
Who from another world my freedom brought,
And to your conquering eyes have lost it here.

CYDARIA - Where is that other world, from whence you came?

CORTEZ - Beyond the ocean, far from hence it lies.

CYDARIA - Your other world, I fear, is then the same,
That souls must go to when the body dies.
But what's the cause that keeps you here with me,
That I may know what keeps me here with you?

CORTEZ - Mine is a love which must perpetual be,
If you can be so just as I am true.

Enter Orbellan.

ORBELLAN - Your father wonders much at your delay.

CYDARIA - So great a wonder for so small a stay!

ORBELLAN - He has commanded you with me to go.

CYDARIA - Has he not sent to bring the stranger too?

ORBELLAN - If he to-morrow dares in fight appear,
His high-placed love perhaps may cost him dear.

CORTEZ - Dares!—that word was never spoke to Spaniard yet,
But forfeited his life, who gave him it;
Haste quickly with thy pledge of safety hence,
Thy guilt's protected by her innocence.

CYDARIA - Sure in some fatal hour my love was born,
So soon o'ercast with absence in the morn!

CORTEZ - Turn hence those pointed glories of your eyes;
For if more charms beneath those circles rise,
So weak my virtue, they so strong appear,
I shall turn ravisher to keep you here.

[Exeunt.

SCENE I—The Magician's Cave

Enter Montezuma, and High-Priest.

MONTEZUMA - Not that I fear the utmost fate can do,
Come I the event of doubtful war to know;
For life and death are things indifferent;
Each to be chose as either brings content:
My motive from a nobler cause does spring,
Love rules my heart, and is your monarch's king;
I more desire to know Almeria's mind,
Than all that heaven has for my state designed.

HIGH PRIEST - By powerful charms, which nothing can withstand,
I'll force the Gods to tell what you demand.

CHARM
Thou moon, that aidest us with thy magic might,
And ye small stars, the scattered seeds of light,
Dart your pale beams into this gloomy place,
That the sad powers of the infernal race
May read above what's hid from human eyes,
And in your walks see empires fall and rise.
And ye, immortal souls, who once were men,
And now, resolved to elements again,
Who wait for mortal frames in depths below,
And did before what we are doomed to do;
Once, twice, and thrice, I wave my sacred wand,
Ascend, ascend, ascend at my command.

[An earthy spirit rises.

SPIRIT - In vain, O mortal men, your prayers implore
The aid of powers below, which want it more:
A God more strong, who all the Gods commands,
Drives us to exile from our native lands;
The air swarms thick with wandering deities,
Which drowsily, like humming beetles, rise
From our loved earth, where peacefully we slept,
And, far from heaven, a long possession kept.
The frighted satyrs, that in woods delight,
Now into plains with pricked-up ears take flight;
And scudding thence, while they their horn-feet ply,
About their sires the little silvans cry.
A nation loving gold must rule this place,
Our temples ruin, and our rites deface:
To them, O king, is thy lost sceptre given.
Now mourn thy fatal search, for since wise heaven

More ill than good to mortals does dispense,
It is not safe to have too quick a sense.
[Descends.

MONTEZUMA - Mourn they, who think repining can remove
The firm decrees of those, who rule above;
The brave are safe within, who still dare die:
Whene'er I fall, I'll scorn my destiny.
Doom as they please my empire not to stand,
I'll grasp my sceptre with my dying hand.

HIGH PRIEST - Those earthy spirits black and envious are;
I'll call up other Gods, of form more fair:
Who visions dress in pleasing colour still,
Set all the good to shew, and hide the ill.
Kalib, ascend, my fair-spoke servant rise,
And sooth my heart with pleasing prophesies.

Kalib ascends all in white, in shape of a woman, and sings.

KALIB - I looked and saw within the book of fate,
Where, many days did lowr,
When lo one happy hour
Leapt up, and smiled to save thy sinking state;
A day shall come when in thy power
Thy cruel foes shall be;
Then shall thy land be free,
And thou in peace shalt reign.
But take, O take that opportunity,
Which, once refused, will never come again.

[Descends.

MONTEZUMA - I shall deserve my fate, if I refuse
That happy hour which heaven allots to use:
But of my crown thou too much care dost take;
That which I value more, my love's at stake.

HIGH PRIEST - Arise, ye subtle spirits, that can spy,
When love is entered in a female's eye;
You, that can read it in the midst of doubt,
And in the midst of frowns can find it out;
You, that can search those many cornered minds,
Where women's crooked fancy turns and winds;
You, that can love explore, and truth impart,
Where both lie deepest hid in woman's heart,
Arise—

[The ghosts of Traxalla and Acacis arise; they stand still, and point at Montezuma.

HIGH PRIEST - I did not for these ghastly visions send;

Their sudden coming does some ill portend.
Begone,—begone,—they will not disappear!
My soul is seized with an unusual fear.

MONTEZUMA - Point on, point on, and see whom you can fright.
Shame and confusion seize these shades of night!
Ye thin and empty forms, am I your sport?

[They smile.

If you were flesh—
You know you durst not use me in this sort.

[The ghost of the Indian Queen rises betwixt the ghosts, with a dagger in her breast.

MONTEZUMA - Ha!
I feel my hair grow stiff, my eye-balls roll!
This is the only form could shake my soul.
Ghost. The hopes of thy successful love resign;
Know, Montezuma, thou art only mine;
For those, who here on earth their passion shew
By death for love, receive their right below.
Why dost thou then delay my longing arms?
Have cares, and age, and mortal life such charms?
The moon grows sickly at the sight of day,
And early cocks have summoned me away:
Yet I'll appoint a meeting place below,
For there fierce winds o'er dusky vallies blow,
Whose every puff bears empty shades away,
Which guidless in those dark dominions stray.
Just at the entrance of the fields below,
Thou shalt behold a tall black poplar grow;
Safe in its hollow trunk I will attend,
And seize thy spirit when thou dost descend.
[Descends.

MONTEZUMA - I'll seize thee there, thou messenger of fate.
Would my short life had yet a shorter date!
I'm weary of this flesh which holds us here,
And dastards manly souls with hope and fear;
These heats and colds still in our breast make war,
Agues and fevers all our passions are. [Exeunt.

SCENE II

Cydaria and Alibech, betwixt the two armies.

ALIBECH - Blessings will crown your name, if you prevent
That blood, which in this battle will be spent;

Nor need you fear so just a suit to move,
Which both becomes your duty and your love.

CYDARIA - But think you he will come? their camp is near,
And he already knows I wait him here.

ALIBECH - You are too young your power to understand,
Lovers take wing upon the least command;
Already he is here.

Enter Cortez and Vasquez to them.

CORTEZ - Methinks, like two black storms on either hand,
Our Spanish army and your Indians stand;
This only space betwixt the clouds is clear,
Where you, like day, broke loose from both appear.

CYDARIA - Those closing skies might still continue bright,
But who can help it, if you'll make it night?
The Gods have given you power of life and death,
Like them to save, or ruin, with a breath.

CORTEZ - That power they to your father did dispose,
'Twas in his choice to make us friends or foes.

ALIBECH - Injurious strength would rapine still excuse,
By offering terms the weaker must refuse;
And such as these your hard conditions are,
You threaten peace, and you invite a war.

CORTEZ - If for myself to conquer here I came,
You might perhaps my actions justly blame:
Now I am sent, and am not to dispute
My prince's orders, but to execute.

ALIBECH - He, who his prince so blindly does obey,
To keep his faith his virtue throws away.

CORTEZ - Monarchs may err; but should each private breast
Judge their ill acts, they would dispute their best.

CYDARIA - Then all your care is for your prince, I see;
Your truth to him out-weighs your love to me:
You may so cruel to deny me prove,
But never after that pretend to love.

CORTEZ - Command my life, and I will soon obey;
To save my honour I my blood will pay.

CYDARIA - What is this honour which does love controul?

CORTEZ - A raging fit of virtue in the soul;
A painful burden which great minds must bear,
Obtained with danger, and possest with fear.

CYDARIA - Lay down that burden if it painful grow;
You'll find, without it, love will lighter go.

CORTEZ - Honour, once lost, is never to be found.

ALIBECH - Perhaps he looks to have both passions crowned;
First dye his honour in a purple flood,
Then court the daughter in the father's blood.

CORTEZ - The edge of war I'll from the battle take,
And spare her father's subjects for her sake.

CYDARIA - I cannot love you less when I'm refused.
But I can die to be unkindly used;
Where shall a maid's distracted heart find rest.
If she can miss it in her lover's breast?

CORTEZ - I till to-morrow will the fight delay;
Remember you have conquered me to-day.

ALIBECH - This grant destroys all you have urged before;
Honour could not give this, or can give more.
Our women in the foremost ranks appear;
March to the fight, and meet your mistress there:
Into the thickest squadrons she must run,
Kill her, and see what honour will be won.

CYDARIA - I must he in the battle, but I'll go
With empty quiver, and unbended bow;
Not draw an arrow in this fatal strife,
For fear its point should reach your noble life.

Enter Pizarro.

CORTEZ - No more: your kindness wounds me to the death:
Honour, be gone! what art thou but a breath?
I'll live, proud of my infamy and shame,
Graced with no triumph but a lover's name;
Men can but say, love did his reason blind,
And love's the noblest frailty of the mind.
Draw off my men; the war's already done.

PIZARRO - Your orders come too late, the fight's begun;
The enemy gives on, with fury led,
And fierce Orbellan combats at their head.

CORTEZ - He justly fears, a peace with me would prove

Of ill concernment to his haughty love;
Retire, fair excellence! I go to meet
New honour, but to lay it at your feet.

[Exeunt Cortez, Vasquez, and Pizarro.]

Enter Odmar and Guyomar, to Alibech and Cydaria.

ODMAR - Now, madam, since a danger does appear
Worthy my courage, though below my fear;
Give leave to him, who may in battle die,
Before his death, to ask his destiny.

GUYOMAR - He cannot die, whom you command to live;
Before the fight, you can the conquest give;
Speak, where you'll place it?

ALIBECH - Briefly, then, to both,
One I in secret love, the other loathe;
But where I hate, my hate I will not show,
And he, I love, my love shall never know;
True worth shall gain me, that it may be said,
Desert, not fancy, once a woman led.
He who, in fight, his courage shall oppose,
With most success, against his country's foes,
From me shall all that recompence receive,
That valour merits, or that love can give.
'Tis true, my hopes and fears are all for one,
But hopes and fears are to myself alone.
Let him not shun the danger of the strife;
I but his love, his country claims his life.

ODMAR - All obstacles my courage shall remove.

GUYOMAR - Fall on, fall on.

ODMAR - For liberty!

GUYOMAR - For love!

[Exeunt, the women following.

SCENE III—Changes to the Indian country

Enter Montezuma, attended by the Indians.

MONTEZUMA - Charge, charge! their ground the faint Taxallans yield!
Bold in close ambush, base in open field.
The envious devil did my fortune wrong:—

Thus fought, thus conquered I, when I was young.

[Exit.

Alarm. Enter Cortez bloody.

CORTEZ - Furies pursue these false Taxallans' flight;
Dare they be friends to us, and dare not fight?
What friends can cowards be, what hopes appear
Of help from such, who, where they hate, show fear!

Enter Pizarro and Vasquez.

PIZARRO - The field grows thin; and those, that now remain,
Appear but like the shadows of the slain.

VASQUEZ - The fierce old king is vanished from the place,
And, in a cloud of dust, pursues the chase.

CORTEZ - Their eager chase disordered does appear,
Command our horse to charge them in the rear:

[To Pizarro.

You to our old Castilian foot retire, [To Vasquez
Who yet stand firm, and at their backs give fire.

[Exeunt severally.

SCENE IV

Enter Odmar and Guyomar, meeting each other in the battle.

ODMAR - Where hast thou been, since first the fight began,
Thou less than woman in the shape of man?

GUYOMAR - Where I have done what may thy envy move,
Things worthy of my birth, and of my love.

ODMAR - Two bold Taxallans with one dart I slew,
And left it sticking ere my sword I drew.

GUYOMAR - I sought not honour on so base a train,
Such cowards by our women may be slain;
I felled along a man of bearded face,
His limbs all covered with a shining case:
So wondrous hard, and so secure of wound,
It made my sword, though edged with flint, re-bound.

ODMAR - I killed a double man; the one half lay
Upon the ground, the other ran away.

[Guns go off within.

Enter Montezuma, out of breath, with him Alibech, and an Indian.

MONTEZUMA - All is lost!—
Our foes with lightning and with thunder fight;
My men in vain shun death by shameful flight:
For deaths invisible come winged with fire,
They hear a dreadful noise, and strait expire.
Take, gods! that soul, ye did in spite create,
And made it great, to be unfortunate:
Ill fate for me unjustly you provide,
Great souls are sparks of your own heavenly pride:
That lust of power we from your godheads have,
You're bound to please those appetites you gave.
Enter Vasquez and Pizarro, with Spaniards.

VASQUEZ - Pizarro, I have hunted hard to-day,
Into our toils, the noblest of the prey;
Seize on the king, and him your prisoner make,
While I, in kind revenge, my taker take.

[Pizarro, with two, goes to attack the king. Vasquez, with another, to seize Alibech.

GUYOMAR - Their danger is alike;—whom shall I free?

ODMAR - I'll follow love!

GUYOMAR - I'll follow piety!

[Odmar retreats from Vasquez, with Alibech, off the stage; Guyomar fights for his father.

GUYOMAR - Fly, sir! while I give back that life you gave;
Mine is well lost, if I your life can save.

[Montezuma fights off; Guyomar, making his retreat, stays.

GUYOMAR - Tis more than man can do to scape them all;
Stay, let me see where noblest I may fall.

[He runs at Vasquez, is seized behind and taken.

VASQUEZ - Conduct him off,
And give command, he strictly guarded be.

GUYOMAR - In vain are guards, death sets the valiant free.

[Exit Guyomar, with guards.

VASQUEZ - A glorious day! and bravely was it fought;
Great fame our general in great dangers sought;
From his strong arm I saw his rival run,
And, in a crowd, the unequal combat shun.
Enter Cortez leading Cydaria, who seems crying and begging of him.

CORTEZ - Man's force is fruitless, and your gods would fail
To save the city, but your tears prevail;
I'll of my fortune no advantage make,
Those terms, they had once given, they still may take.

CYDARIA - Heaven has of right all victory designed,
Where boundless power dwells in a will confined;
Your Spanish honour does the world excel.

CORTEZ - Our greatest honour is in loving well.

CYDARIA - Strange ways you practise there, to win a heart;
Here love is nature, but with you 'tis art.

CORTEZ - Love is with us as natural as here,
But fettered up with customs more severe.
In tedious courtship we declare our pain,
And, ere we kindness find, first meet disdain.

CYDARIA - If women love, they needless pains endure;
Their pride and folly but delay their cure.

CORTEZ - What you miscall their folly, is their care;
They know how fickle common lovers are:
Their oaths and vows are cautiously believed,
For few there are but have been once deceived.

CYDARIA - But if they are not trusted when they vow,
What other marks of passion can they show?

CORTEZ - With feasts, and music, all that brings delight,
Men treat their ears, their palates, and their sight.

CYDARIA - Your gallants, sure, have little eloquence,
Failing to move the soul, they court the sense:
With pomp, and trains, and in a crowd they woo,
When true felicity is but in two;
But can such toys your women's passions move?
This is but noise and tumult, 'tis not love.

CORTEZ - I have no reason, madam, to excuse
Those ways of gallantry, I did not use;
My love was true, and on a nobler score.

CYDARIA - Your love, alas! then have you loved before?

CORTEZ - 'Tis true I loved, but she is dead, she's dead;
And I should think with her all beauty fled,
Did not her fair resemblance live in you,
And, by that image, my first flames renew.

CYDARIA - Ah! happy beauty, whosoe'er thou art!
Though dead, thou keep'st possession of his heart;
Thou makest me jealous to the last degree,
And art my rival in his memory:
Within his memory! ah, more than so,
Thou livest and triumph'st o'er Cydaria too.

CORTEZ - What strange disquiet has uncalmed your breast,
Inhuman fair, to rob the dead of rest!—
Poor heart! she slumbers in her silent tomb;
Let her possess in peace that narrow room.

CYDARIA - Poor heart!—he pities and bewails her death!—
Some god, much hated soul, restore thy breath,
That I may kill thee; but, some ease 'twill be,
I'll kill myself for but resembling thee.

CORTEZ - I dread your anger, your disquiet fear,
But blows, from hands so soft, who would not bear?
So kind a passion why should I remove?
Since jealousy but shows how well we love.
Yet jealousy so strange I never knew;
Can she, who loves me not, disquiet you?
For in the grave no passions fill the breast,
'Tis all we gain by death, to be at rest.

CYDARIA - That she no longer loves, brings no relief;
Your love to her still lives, and that's my grief.

CORTEZ - The object of desire once ta'en away,
'Tis then not love, but pity, which we pay.

CYDARIA - 'Tis such a pity I should never have,
When I must lie forgotten in the grave;
I meant to have obliged you, when I died,
That, after me, you should love none beside.—
But you are false already.

CORTEZ - If untrue,
By heaven! my falsehood is to her, not you.

CYDARIA - Observe, sweet heaven, how falsely he does swear!—
You said, you loved me for resembling her.

CORTEZ - That love was in me by resemblance bred,
But shows you cheared my sorrows for the dead.

CYDARIA - You still repeat the greatness of your grief.

CORTEZ - If that was great, how great was the relief!

CYDARIA - The first love still the strongest we account.

CORTEZ - That seems more strong which could the first surmount:
But if you still continue thus unkind,
Whom I love best, you, by my death, shall find.

CYDARIA - If you should die, my death shall yours pursue;
But yet I am not satisfied you're true.

CORTEZ - Hear me, ye gods! and punish him you hear,
If aught within the world I hold so dear.

CYDARIA - You would deceive the gods and me; she's dead,
And is not in the world, whose love I dread.—
Name not the world; say, nothing is so dear.

CORTEZ - Then nothing is,—let that secure your fear.

CYDARIA - 'Tis time must wear it off, but I must go.
Can you your constancy in absence show?

CORTEZ - Misdoubt my constancy, and do not try,
But stay, and keep me ever in your eye.

CYDARIA - If as a prisoner I were here, you might
Have then insisted on a conqueror's right,
And staid me here; but now my love would be
The effect of force, and I would give it free.

CORTEZ - To doubt your virtue, or your love, were sin!
Call for the captive prince, and bring him in.

Enter Guyomar, bound and sad.

You look, sir, as your fate you could not bear:

[To GUYOMAR

Are Spanish fetters, then, so hard to wear?
Fortune's unjust, she ruins oft the brave,
And him, who should be victor, makes the slave.

GUYOMAR - Son of the sun! my fetters cannot be
But glorious for me, since put on by thee;

The ills of love, not those of fate, I fear;
These can I brave, but those I cannot bear:
My rival brother, while I'm held in chains,
In freedom reaps the fruit of all my pains.

CORTEZ - Let it be never said that he, whose breast
Is filled with love, should break a lover's rest.
Haste! lose no time!—your sister sets you free:
And tell the king, my generous enemy,
I offer still those terms he had before,
Only ask leave his daughter to adore.

GUYOMAR - Brother, (that name my breast shall ever own,
[He embraces him.
The name of foe be but in battles known;)
For some few days all hostile acts forbear,
That, if the king consents, it seem not fear:
His heart, is noble, and great souls must be
Most sought and courted in adversity.—
Three days, I hope, the wished success will tell.

CYDARIA - Till that long time,—

CORTEZ - Till that long time, farewell.

[Exeunt severally.

ACT III

SCENE I—A Chamber Royal

Enter Odmar and Alibech.

ODMAR - The gods, fair Alibech, had so decreed,
Nor could my valour against fate succeed;
Yet though our army brought not conquest home,
I did not from the fight inglorious come:
If, as a victor, you the brave regard,
Successless courage, then, may hope reward;
And I, returning safe, may justly boast,
To win the prize which my dear brother lost.

Enter Guyomar behind him.

GUYOMAR - No, no, thy brother lives! and lives to be
A witness, both against himself and thee;
Though both in safety are returned again,
I blush to ask her love for vanquished men.

ODMAR - Brother, I'll not dispute but you are brave;
Yet I was free, and you, it seems, a slave.

GUYOMAR - Odmar, 'tis true that I was captive led;
As publicly 'tis known, as that you fled:
But of two shames, if she must one partake,
I think the choice will not be hard to make.

ODMAR - Freedom and bondage in her choice remain;
Darest thou expect she will put on thy chain?

GUYOMAR - No, no, fair Alibech, give him the crown,
My brother is returned with high renown:
He thinks by flight his mistress must be won,
And claims the prize, because he best did run.

ALIBECH - Your chains were glorious, and your flight was wise,
But neither have o'ercome your enemies:
My secret wishes would my choice decide,
But open justice bends to neither side.

ODMAR - Justice already does my right approve,
If him, who loves you most, you most should love.
My brother poorly from your aid withdrew,
But I my father left, to succour you.

GUYOMAR - Her country she did to herself prefer,
Him who fought best, not who defended her;
Since she her interest, for the nation's, waved,
Then I, who saved the king, the nation saved.
You, aiding her, your country did betray;
I, aiding him, did her commands obey.

ODMAR - Name it no more; in love there is a time
When dull obedience is the greatest crime.
She to her country's use resigned your sword,
And you, kind lover, took her at her word;
You did your duty to your love prefer,
Seek your reward from duty, not from her.

GUYOMAR - In acting what my duty did require,
'Twas hard for me to quit my own desire;
That fought for her, which, when I did subdue,
'Twas much the easier task I left to you.

ALIBECH - Odmar a more than common love has shown,
And Guyomar's was greater, or was none;
Which I should chuse, some god direct my breast.
The certain good, or the uncertain best. —
I cannot chuse, — you both dispute in vain, —

Time and your future acts must make it plain;
First raise the siege, and set your country free,
I, not the judge, but the reward, will be.
To them,

Enter Montezuma, talking with Almeria and Orbellan.

MONTEZUMA - Madam, I think, with reason, I extol
The virtue of the Spanish general;
When all the gods our ruin have foretold,
Yet generously he does his arms withhold,
And, offering peace, the first conditions make.

ALMERIA - When peace is offered, 'tis too late to take;
For one poor loss, to stoop to terms like those! —
Were we o'ercome, what could they worse impose?
Go, go, with homage your proud victors meet!
Go, lie like dogs beneath your masters' feet!
Go, and beget them slaves to dig their mines,
And groan for gold, which now in temples shines!
Your shameful story shall record of me,
The men all crouched, and left a woman free!

GUYOMAR - Had I not fought, or durst not fight again,
I my suspected counsel should refrain;
For I wish peace, and any terms prefer,
Before the last extremities of war.
We but exasperate those we cannot harm,
And fighting gains us but to die more warm:
If that be cowardice, which dares not see
The insolent effects of victory,
The rape of matrons, and their childrens cries, —
Then I am fearful, let the brave advise.

ODMAR - Keen cutting swords, and engines killing far,
Have prosperously begun a doubtful war:
But now our foes with less advantage fight,
Their strength decreases with our Indians' fright.

MONTEZUMA - This noble vote does with my wish comply, I am for war.

ALMERIA - And so am I.

ORBELLAN - And I.

MONTEZUMA - Then send to break the truce, and I'll take care To chear the soldiers, and for fight prepare.

[Exeunt Montezuma, Odmar, Guyomar and Alibech.

ALMERIA [to Orbellan] 'Tis now the hour which all to rest allow,

And sleep sits heavy upon every brow;
In this dark silence softly leave the town,

[Guyomar returns, and hears them.

And to the general's tent,—'tis quickly known,
Direct your steps: You may despatch him: strait,
Drowned in his sleep, and easy for his fate:
Besides, the truce will make the guards more slack.

ORBELLAN - Courage, which leads me on, will bring me back.
But I more fear the baseness of the thing:
Remorse, you know, bears a perpetual sting.

ALMERIA - For mean remorse no room the valiant find,
Repentance is the virtue of weak minds;
For want of judgment keeps them doubtful still,
They may repent of good, who can of ill;
But daring courage makes ill actions good,
'Tis foolish pity spares a rival's blood;
You shall about it strait.

[Exeunt Almeria and Orbellan

GUYOMAR - Would they betray
His sleeping virtue, by so mean a way!
And yet this Spaniard is our nation's foe,
I wish him dead,—but cannot wish it so;
Either my country never must be freed,
Or I consenting to so black a deed.
Would chance had never led my steps this way!
Now if he dies, I murder him, not they;
Something must be resolved ere 'tis too late;
He gave me freedom, I'll prevent his fate.

[Exit.

SCENE II—A Camp

Enter Cortez alone, in a night-gown.

CORTEZ - All things are hushed, as nature's self lay dead;
The mountains seem to nod their drowsy head;
The little birds, in dreams, their songs repeat,
And sleeping flowers beneath the night-dew sweat.
Even lust and envy sleep; yet love denies
Rest to my soul, and slumber to my eyes.
Three days I promised to attend my doom,
And two long days and nights are yet to come:

'Tis sure the noise of some tumultuous fight,

[Noise within.

They break the truce, and sally out by night.

Enter Orbellan, flying in the dark, his sword drawn.

ORBELLAN - Betrayed! pursued! O, whither shall I fly?
See, see! the just reward of treachery!—
I'm sure among the tents, but know not where;
Even night wants darkness to secure my fear.

[Comes near Cortez, who hears him.

CORTEZ - Stand! who goes there?

ORBELLAN - Alas, what shall I say?

[Aside.

A poor Taxallan that mistook his way,
And wanders in the terrors of the night.

CORTEZ - Soldier, thou seem'st afraid; whence comes thy fright?

ORBELLAN - The insolence of Spaniards caused my fear,
Who in the dark pursued me entering here.

CORTEZ - Their crimes shall meet immediate punishment,
But stay thou safe within the general's tent.

ORBELLAN - Still worse and worse.

CORTEZ - Fear not, but follow me;
Upon my life I'll set thee safe and free.

[Cortez leads him in, and returns.

To him Vasquez, Pizarro, and Spaniards with Torches.

VASQUEZ - O sir, thank heaven, and your brave Indian friend,
That you are safe; Orbellan did intend
This night to kill you sleeping in your tent:
But Guyomar his trusty slave has sent,
Who, following close his silent steps by night,
Till in our camp they both approached the light,
Cried-Seize the traitor, seize the murtherer!
The cruel villain fled I know not where;
But far he is not, for he this way bent.

PIZARRO - The enraged soldiers seek, from tent to tent,
With lighted torches, and in love to you,
With bloody vows his hated life pursue.

VASQUEZ - This messenger does, since he came, relate,
That the old king, after a long debate,
By his imperious mistress blindly led,
Has given Cydaria to Orbellan's bed.

CORTEZ - Vasquez, the trusty slave with you retain;
Retire a while, I'll call you back again.

[Exeunt Vasquez and Pizarro

CORTEZ [at his tent door] -
Indian, come forth; your enemies are gone,
And I, who saved you from them, here alone.

Enter Orbellan, holding his face aside.

You hide your face, as you were still afraid:
Dare you not look on him, who gave you aid?

ORBELLAN - Moon, slip behind some cloud, some tempest, rise,
And blow out all the stars that light the skies,
To shroud my shame!

CORTEZ - In vain you turn aside,
And hide your face; your name you cannot hide:
I know my rival and his black design.

ORBELLAN - Forgive it, as my passion's fault, not mine.

CORTEZ - In your excuse your love does little say;
You might, howe'er, have took a fairer way.

ORBELLAN - 'Tis true, my passion small defence can make;
Yet you must spare me for your honour's sake,
That was engaged to set me safe and free.

CORTEZ - 'Twas to a stranger, not an enemy:
Nor is it prudence to prolong thy breath,
When all my hopes depend upon thy death;
Yet none shall tax me with base perjury:
Something I'll do, both for myself and thee;
With vowed revenge my soldiers search each tent,
If thou art seen, none can thy death prevent;
Follow my steps with silence and with haste.

SCENE III

They go out, the Scene changes to the Indian Country, they return.

CORTEZ - Now you are safe, you have my outguards past.

ORBELLAN - Then here I take my leave.

CORTEZ - Orbellan, no;
When you return, you to Cydaria go:
I'll send a message.

ORBELLAN - Let it be exprest;
I am in haste.

CORTEZ - I'll write it in your breast.

[Draws.

ORBELLAN - What means my rival?

CORTEZ - Either fight or die,
I'll not strain honour to a point too high;
I saved your life, and keep it if you can,
Cydaria shall be for the bravest man;
On equal terms you shall your fortune try,
Take this, and lay your flint-edged weapon by;

[Gives him a sword.

I'll arm you for my glory, and pursue
No palm, but what's to manly virtue due.
Fame, with my conquest, shall my courage tell.
This you shall gain, by placing love so well.

ORBELLAN - Fighting with you, ungrateful I appear.

CORTEZ - Under that shadow, thou would'st hide thy fear:
Thou would'st possess thy love at thy return,
And in her arms my easy virtue scorn.

ORBELLAN - Since we must fight, no longer let's delay;
The moon shines clear, and makes a paler day.

[They fight, Orbellan is wounded in the hand, his sword falls out of it.

CORTEZ - To courage, even of foes, there's pity due;
It was not I, but fortune, vanquished you:

[Throws his sword again.

Thank me with that, and so dispute the prize,
As if you fought before Cydaria's eyes.

ORBELLAN - I would not poorly such a gift requite;
You gave me not this sword to yield, but fight:
[He strives to hold it, but cannot.
But see, where yours has forced its bloody way;
My wounded hand my heart does ill obey.

CORTEZ - Unlucky honour, that controul'st my will?
Why have I vanquished, since I must not kill?
Fate sees thy life lodged in a brittle glass,
And looks it through, but to it cannot pass.

ORBELLAN - All I can do is frankly to confess,
I wish I could, but cannot, love her less:
To swear I would resign her, were but vain,
Love would recal that perjured breath again;
And in my wretched case, 'twill be more just,
Not to have promised, than deceive your trust.
Know, if I live once more to see the town,
In bright Cydaria's arms my love I'll crown.

CORTEZ - In spite of that, I give thee liberty,
And with thy person leave thy honour free;
But to thy wishes move a speedy pace,
Or death will soon o'ertake thee in the chase.—
To arms, to arms; fate shows my love the way,
I'll force the city on thy nuptial day.

[Exeunt severally.

SCENE IV—Mexico

Enter Montezuma, Odmar, Guyomar, Almeria.

MONTEZUMA - It moves my wonder, that in two days space,
This early famine spreads so swift a pace.

ODMAR - 'Tis, sir, the general cry; nor seems it strange,
The face of plenty should so swiftly change:
This city never felt a siege before,
But from the lake received its daily store;
Which now shut up, and millions crowded here,
Famine will soon in multitudes appear.

MONTEZUMA - The more the number, still the greater shame.

ALMERIA - What if some one should seek immortal fame,

By ending of the siege at one brave blow?

MONTEZUMA - That were too happy!

ALMERIA - Yet it may be so.
What if the Spanish general should be slain?

GUYOMAR - Just heavens I hope, does otherwise ordain.

[Aside.

MONTEZUMA - If slain by treason, I lament his death.

Enter Orbellan, and whispers his sister.

ODMAR - Orbellan seems in haste, and out of breath.

MONTEZUMA - Orbellan, welcome; you are early here,
A bridegroom's haste does in your looks appear.

[Almeria aside to her brother.

ALMERIA - Betrayed! no, 'twas thy cowardice and fear;
He had not 'scaped with life, had I been there:
But since so ill you act a brave design,
Keep close your shame;—fate makes the next turn mine.

Enter Alibech and Cydaria.

ALIBECH - O sir, if ever pity touched your breast,
Let it be now to your own blood exprest:
In tears your beauteous daughter drowns her sight,
Silent as dews that fall in dead of night.

CYDARIA - To your commands I strict obedience owe,
And my last act of it I come to show:
I want the heart to die before your eyes,
But grief will finish that which fear denies.

ALMERIA - Your will should by your father's precept move.

CYDARIA - When he was young, he taught me truth in love.

ALMERIA - He found more love than he deserved, 'tis true,
And that, it seems, is lucky too to you;
Your father's folly took a headstrong course,
But I'll rule yours, and teach you love by force.
Enter Messenger.

MESSENGER - Arm, arm, O king! the enemy comes on,
A sharp assault already is begun;

Their murdering guns play fiercely on the walls.

ODMAR - Now, rival, let us run where honour calls.

GUYOMAR - I have discharged what gratitude did owe,
And the brave Spaniard is again my foe.

[Exeunt Odmar and Guyomar.

MONTEZUMA - Our walls are high, and multitudes defend:
Their vain attempt must in their ruin end;
The nuptials with my presence shall be graced.

ALIBECH - At least but stay 'till the assault be past.

ALMERIA - Sister, in vain you urge him to delay,
The king has promised, and he shall obey.

Enter second Messenger.

SECOND MESSENGER - From several parts the enemy's repelled,
One only quarter to the assault does yield.

Enter third Messenger.

THIRD MESSENGER - Some foes are entered, but they are so few,
They only death, not victory, pursue.

ORBELLAN - Hark, hark, they shout!
From virtue's rules I do too meanly swerve,
I, by my courage, will your love deserve.

[Exit.

MONTEZUMA - Here, in the heart of all the town, I'll stay;
And timely succour, where it wants, convey.

A noise within. Enter Orbellan, Indians driven in, Cortez after them, and one or two Spaniards.

CORTEZ - He's found, he's found! degenerate coward, stay:
Night saved thee once, thou shalt not scape by day.

[Kills Orbellan.

ORBELLAN - O, I am killed—

[Dies.

Enter Guyomar and Odmar.

GUYOMAR - Yield, generous stranger, and preserve your life;

Why chuse you death in this unequal strife?

[He is beset.

[Almeria and Alibech fall on Orbellan's body.

CORTEZ - What nobler fate could any lover meet?
I fall revenged, and at my mistress' feet.

[They fall on him, and bear him down, Guyomar takes his sword.

ALIBECH - He's past recovery; my dear brother's slain,
Fate's hand was in it, and my care is vain.

ALMERIA - In weak complaints you vainly waste your breath:
They are not tears that can revenge his death.
Despatch the villain strait.

CORTEZ - The villain's dead.

ALMERIA - Give me a sword, and let me take his head.

MONTEZUMA - Though, madam, for your brother's loss I grieve, Yet let me beg—

ALMERIA - His murderer may live?

CYDARIA - 'Twas his misfortune, and the chance of war.

CORTEZ - It was my purpose, and I killed him fair:
How could you so unjust and cruel prove,
To call that chance, which was the act of love?

CYDARIA - I called it any thing to save your life:
Would he were living still, and I his wife!
That wish was once my greatest misery:
But 'tis a greater to behold you die.

ALMERIA - Either command his death upon the place,
Or never more behold Almeria's face.

GUYOMAR - You by his valour once from death were freed:
Can you forget so generous a deed?

[To Montezuma.

Montezuma - How gratitude and love divide my breast!
Both ways alike my soul is robbed of rest.
But—let him die—Can I his sentence give?
Ungrateful, must he die, by whom I live?
But can I then Almeria's tears deny?
Should any live whom she commands to die?

GUYOMAR - Approach who dares: He yielded on my word;
And, as my prisoner, I restore his sword.

[Gives his sword.

His life concerns the safety of the state,
And I'll preserve it for a calm debate.

MONTEZUMA - Dar'st thou rebel, false and degenerate boy?
That being, which I gave, I thus destroy.

[Offers to kill him, Odmar steps between.

ODMAR - My brother's blood I cannot see you spill,
Since he prevents you but from doing ill.
He is my rival, but his death would be
For him too glorious, and too base for me.

GUYOMAR - Thou shalt not conquer in this noble strife:
Alas, I meant not to defend my life:
Strike, sir, you never pierced a breast more true;
'Tis the last wound I e'er can take for you.
You see I live but to dispute your will;
Kill me, and then you may my prisoner kill.

CORTEZ - You shall not, generous youths, contend for me:
It is enough that I your honour see:
But that your duty may no blemish take,
I will myself your father's captive make:

[Gives his sword to Montezuma.

When he dares strike, I am prepared to fall:
The Spaniards will revenge their general.

CYDARIA - Ah, you too hastily your life resign,
You more would love it, if you valued mine!

CORTEZ - Despatch me quickly, I my death forgive;
I shall grow tender else, and wish to live;
Such an infectious face her sorrow wears,
I can bear death, but not Cydaria's tears.

ALMERIA - Make haste, make haste, they merit death all three:
They for rebellion, and for murder he.
See, see, my brother's ghost hangs hovering there
O'er his warm blood, that steams into the air;
Revenge, revenge, it cries.

MONTEZUMA - And it shall have;

But two days respite for his life I crave:
If in that space you not more gentle prove,
I'll give a fatal proof how well I love.
'Till when, you, Guyomar, your prisoner take;
Bestow him in the castle on the lake:
In that small time I shall the conquest gain
Of these few sparks of virtue which remain;
Then all, who shall my headlong passion see,
Shall curse my crimes, and yet shall pity me.

[Exeunt.

ACT IV

SCENE I—A Prison

Enter Almeria and an Indian; they speak entering.

INDIAN - A dangerous proof of my respect I show.

ALMERIA - Fear not, Prince Guyomar shall never know:
While he is absent let us not delay;
Remember 'tis the king thou dost obey.

INDIAN - See where he sleeps.

[Cortez appears chained and laid asleep.

ALMERIA - Without, my coming wait;
And, on thy life, secure the prison gate.

[Exit Indian.

[She plucks out a dagger, and approaches him.

Spaniard, awake: thy fatal hour is come:
Thou shalt not at such ease receive thy doom.
Revenge is sure, though sometimes slowly paced:
Awake, awake, or, sleeping, sleep thy last.

CORTEZ - Who names revenge?

ALMERIA - Look up, and thou shalt see.

CORTEZ - I cannot fear so fair an enemy.

ALMERIA - No aid is nigh, nor canst thou make defence:
Whence can thy courage come?

CORTEZ - From innocence.

ALMERIA - From innocence? let that then take thy part.
Still are thy looks assured—have at thy heart!

[Holds up the dagger.

I cannot kill thee; sure thou bear'st some charm,

[Goes back.

Or some divinity holds back my arm.
Why do I thus delay to make him bleed?

[Aside.

Can I want courage for so brave a deed?
I've shook it off; my soul is free from fear.

[Comes again.

And I can now strike any where—but here:
His scorn of death, how strangely does it move!
A mind so haughty who could chuse but love!

[Goes off.

Plead not a charm, or any god's command,
Alas, it is thy heart that holds thy hand:
In spite of me I love, and see, too late,
My mother's pride must find my mother's fate.
Thy country's foe, thy brother's murderer,—
For shame, Almeria, such mad thoughts forbear:
It w'onnot be,—if I once more come on,

[Coming on again.

I shall mistake the breast, and pierce my own.

[Comes with her dagger down.

CORTEZ - Does your revenge maliciously forbear
To give me death, 'till 'tis prepared by fear?
If you delay for that, forbear or strike,
Foreseen and sudden death are both alike.

ALMERIA - To show my love would but increase his pride:
They have most power, who most their passions hide.

[Aside.

Spaniard, I must confess, I did expect
You could not meet your death with such neglect;
I will defer it now, and give you time:
You may repent, and I forget your crime.

CORTEZ - Those, who repent, acknowledge they do ill:
I did not unprovoked your brother kill.

ALMERIA - Petition me, perhaps I may forgive.

CORTEZ - Who begs his life does not deserve to live.

ALMERIA - But if 'tis given, you'll not refuse to take?

CORTEZ - I can live gladly for Cydaria's sake.

ALMERIA - Does she so wholly then possess your mind?
What if you should another lady find,
Equal to her in birth, and far above
In all that can attract, or keep your love,
Would you so doat upon your first desire,
As not to entertain a nobler fire?

CORTEZ - I think that person hardly will be found,
With gracious form and equal virtue crowned:
Yet if another could precedence claim,
My fixed desires could find no fairer aim.

ALMERIA - Dull ignorance! he cannot yet conceive:
To speak more plain, shame will not give me leave.

[Aside.

Suppose one loved you, whom even kings adore:

[To him.

Who, with your life, your freedom would restore,
And add to that the crown of Mexico:
Would you, for her, Cydaria's love forego?

CORTEZ - Though she could offer all you can invent,
I could not of my faith, once vowed, repent.

ALMERIA - A burning blush has covered all my face;
Why am I forced to publish my disgrace?
What if I love? you know it cannot be,
And yet I blush to put the case—'twere me.
If I could love you with a flame so true,
I could forget what hand my brother slew—
Make out the rest—I am disordered so,

I know not farther what to say or do:
But answer me to what you think I meant.

CORTEZ - Reason or wit no answer can invent:
Of words confused who can the meaning find?

ALMERIA - Disordered words show a distempered mind.

CORTEZ - She has obliged me so, that could I chuse,
I would not answer what I must refuse. [Aside.

ALMERIA - His mind is shook—suppose I loved you, speak,
Would you for me Cydaria's fetters break?

CORTEZ - Things, meant in jest, no serious answer need.

ALMERIA - But, put the case that it were so indeed.

CORTEZ - If it were so,—which but to think were pride,—
My constant love would dangerously be tried:
For since you could a brother's death forgive,
He, whom you save, for you alone should live:
But I, the most unhappy of mankind,
Ere I knew yours, have all my love resigned:
'Tis my own loss I grieve, who have no more:
You go a-begging to a bankrupt's door.
Yet could I change, as sure I never can,
How could you love so infamous a man?
For love, once given from her, and placed in you,
Would leave no ground I ever could be true.

ALMERIA - You construed me aright—I was in jest:
And, by that offer, meant to sound your breast;
Which since I find so constant to your love,
Will much my value of your worth improve.
Spaniard, assure yourself you shall not be
Obliged to quit Cydaria for me:
'Tis dangerous though to treat me in this sort,
And to refuse my offers, though in sport. [Exit.

CORTEZ - In what a strange condition am I left?
More than I wish I have, of all I wish bereft!
In wishing nothing, we enjoy still most;
For even our wish is, in possession, lost:
Restless, we wander to a new desire,
And burn ourselves, by blowing up the fire:
We toss and turn about our feverish will,
When all our ease must come by lying still:
For all the happiness mankind can gain
Is not in pleasure, but in rest from pain.

[Goes in, and the scene closes upon him.

SCENE II—Chamber-royal

Enter Montezuma, Odmar, Guyomar, and Alibech.

MONTEZUMA - My ears are deaf with this impatient crowd.

ODMAR - Their wants are now grown mutinous and loud:
The general's taken, but the siege remains;
And their last food our dying men sustains.

GUYOMAR - One means is only left. I to this hour
Have kept the captive from Almeria's power;
And though, by your command, she often sent
To urge his doom, do still his death prevent.

MONTEZUMA - That hope is past: Him I have oft assailed;
But neither threats nor kindness have prevailed;
Hiding our wants, I offered to release
His chains, and equally conclude a peace:
He fiercely answered, I had now no way
But to submit, and without terms obey:
I told him, he in chains demanded more
Than he imposed in victory before:
He sullenly replied, he could not make
These offers now; honour must give, not take.

ODMAR - Twice have I sallied, and was twice beat back:
What desp'rate course remains for us to take!

MONTEZUMA - If either death or bondage I must chuse,
I'll keep my freedom, though my life I lose.

GUYOMAR - I'll not upbraid you, that you once refused
Those means, you might have then with honour used;
I'll lead your men, perhaps bring victory:
They know to conquer best, who know to die.

[Exeunt Montezuma and Odmar.

ALIBECH - Ah me, what have I heard! stay, Guyomar,
What hope you from this sally you prepare?

GUYOMAR - A death, with honour, for my country's good:
A death, to which yourself designed my blood.

ALIBECH - You heard, and I well know the town's distress,
Which sword and famine both at once oppress:

Famine so fierce, that what's denied man's use,
Even deadly plants, and herbs of poisonous juice,
Wild hunger seeks; and, to prolong our breath,
We greedily devour our certain death:
The soldier in th' assault of famine falls:
And ghosts, not men, are watching on the walls.
As callow birds—
Whose mother's killed in seeking of the prey,
Cry in their nest, and think her long away;
And at each leaf that stirs, each blast of wind,
Gape for the food, which they must never find:
So cry the people in their misery.

GUYOMAR - And what relief can they expect from me?

ALIBECH - While Montezuma sleeps, call in the foe:
The captive general your design may know:
His noble heart, to honour ever true,
Knows how to spare as well as to subdue.

GUYOMAR - What I have heard I blush to hear: And grieve,
Those words you spoke I must your words believe.
I to do this! I, whom you once thought brave,
To sell my country, and my king enslave?
All I have done by one foul act deface,
And yield my right to you, by turning base?
What more could Odmar wish that I should do,
To lose your love, than you persuade me to?
No, madam, no, I never can commit
A deed so ill, nor can you suffer it:
'Tis but to try what virtue you can find
Lodged in my soul.

ALIBECH - I plainly speak my mind;
Dear as my life my virtue I'll preserve,
But virtue you too scrupulously serve:
I loved not more than now my country's good,
When for its service I employed your blood:
But things are altered, I am still the same,
By different ways still moving to one fame;
And by disarming you, I now do more
To save the town, than arming you before.

GUYOMAR - Things good or ill by circumstances be,
In you 'tis virtue, what is vice in me.

ALIBECH - That ill is pardoned, which does good procure.

GUYOMAR - The good's uncertain, but the ill is sure.

ALIBECH - When kings grow stubborn, slothful, or unwise,

Each private man for public good should rise.

GUYOMAR - Take heed, fair maid, how monarchs you accuse:
Such reasons none but impious rebels use:
Those, who to empire by dark paths aspire,
Still plead a call to what they most desire;
But kings by free consent their kingdoms take,
Strict as those sacred ties which nuptials make;
And whate'er faults in princes time reveal,
None can be judge where can be no appeal.

ALIBECH - In all debates you plainly let me see
You love your virtue best, but Odmar me:
Go, your mistaken piety pursue:
I'll have from him what is denied by you;
With my commands you shall no more be graced.
Remember, sir, this trial was your last.

GUYOMAR - The gods inspire you with a better mind;
Make you more just, and make you then more kind!
But though from virtue's rules I cannot part,
Think I deny you with a bleeding heart:
'Tis hard with me whatever choice I make;
I must not merit you, or must forsake:
But, in this strait, to honour I'll be true,
And leave my fortune to the gods and you.

Enter Messenger privately.

MESSENGER - Now is the time; be aiding to your fate;
From the watch-tower, above the western-gate,
I have discerned the foe securely lie,
Too proud to fear a beaten enemy:
Their careless chiefs to the cool grottoes run,
The bowers of kings, to shade them from the sun.

GUYOMAR - Upon thy life disclose thy news to none;
I'll make the conquest or the shame my own.

[Exeunt Guyomar and Messenger.

Enter Odmar.

ALIBECH - I read some welcome message in his eye:
Prince Odmar comes: I'll see if he'll deny.
Odmar, I come to tell you pleasing news;
I begged a thing, your brother did refuse.

ODMAR - The news both pleases me, and grieves me too;
For nothing, sure, should be denied to you:
But he was blessed who might commanded be;

You never meant that happiness to me.

ALIBECH - What he refused, your kindness might bestow,
But my commands, perhaps, your burden grow.

ODMAR - Could I but live till burdensome they prove,
My life would be immortal as my love.
Your wish, ere it receive a name, I grant.

ALIBECH - 'Tis to relieve your dying country's want;
All hopes of succour from your arms is past,
To save us now you must our ruin haste;
Give up the town, and, to oblige him more.
The captive general's liberty restore.

ODMAR - You speak to try my love; can you forgive
So soon, to let your brother's murderer live?

ALIBECH - Orbellan, though my brother, did disgrace,
With treacherous deeds, our mighty mother's race;
And to revenge his blood, so justly spilt,
What is it less than to partake his guilt?
Though my proud sister to revenge incline,
I to my country's good my own resign.

ODMAR - To save our lives, our freedom I betray—
Yet, since I promised it, I will obey;
I'll not my shame nor your commands dispute;
You shall behold your empire's absolute. [Exit.

ALIBECH - I should have thanked him for his speedy grant,
And yet, I know not how, fit words I want:
Sure I am grown distracted in my mind;—
That joy, this grant should bring, I cannot find:
The one, denying, vexed my soul before;
And this, obeying, has disturbed me more:
The one, with grief, and slowly, did refuse,
The other, in his grant, much haste did use:
He used too much—and, granting me so soon,
He has the merit of the gift undone:
Methought with wondrous ease he swallowed down
His forfeit honour, to betray the town:
My inward choice was Guyomar before,
But now his virtue has confirmed me more—
I rave, I rave, for Odmar will obey,
And then my promise must my choice betray.
Fantastic honour, thou hast framed a toil
Thyself, to make thy love thy virtue's spoil. [Exit.

SCENE III

A pleasant grotto discovered; in it a fountain spouting; round about it Vasquez, Pizarro, and other Spaniards, lying carelessly unarmed, and by them many Indian women, one of which sings the following song.

SONG.
Ah fading joy! how quickly art thou past!
Yet we thy ruin haste.
As if the cares of human life were few,
We seek out new:
And follow fate, which would too fast pursue.
See, how on every bough the birds express,
In their sweet notes, their happiness.
They all enjoy, and nothing spare;
But on their mother nature lay their care:
Why then should man, the lord of all below,
Such troubles chuse to know,
As none of all his subjects undergo?
Hark, hark, the waters, fall, fall, fall,
And with a murmuring sound
Dash, dash, upon the ground,
To gentle slumbers call.

After the song two Spaniards arise, and dance a saraband with castanietas: At the end of which Guyomar and his Indians enter, and, ere the Spaniards can recover their swords, seize them.

GUYOMAR - Those, whom you took without, in triumph bring;
But see these strait conducted to the king.

PIZARRO - Vasquez, what now remains in these extremes?

VASQUEZ - Only to wake us from our golden dreams.

PIZARRO - Since by our shameful conduct we have lost
Freedom, wealth, honour, which we value most,
I wish they would our lives a period give:
They live too long, who happiness out-live.

[Spaniards are led out.

FIRST INDIAN - See, sir, how quickly your success is spread;
The king comes marching in the army's head.

Enter Montezuma, Alibech, Odmar discontented.

MONTEZUMA - Now all the Gods reward and bless my son. [Embracing.
Thou hast this day thy father's youth outdone.

ALIBECH - Just heaven all happiness upon him shower,
Till it confess its will beyond its power.

GUYOMAR - The heavens are kind, the Gods propitious be,
I only doubt a mortal deity:
I neither fought for Conquest, nor for fame,
Your love alone can recompence my flame.

ALIBECH - I gave my love to the most brave in war;
But that the king must judge.

MONTEZUMA - 'Tis Guyomar.

[Soldiers shout, A Guyomar, &c.

MONTEZUMA - This day your nuptials we will celebrate;
But guard these haughty captives 'till their fate:
Odmar, this night to keep them be your care,
To-morrow for their sacrifice prepare.

ALIBECH - Blot not your conquest with your cruelty.

MONTEZUMA - Fate says, we are not safe unless they die:
The spirit, that foretold this happy day,
Bid me use caution and avoid delay:
Posterity be juster to my fame;
Nor call it murder, when each private man
In his defence may justly do the same:
But private persons more than monarchs can:
All weigh our acts, and whate'er seems unjust,
Impute not to necessity, but lust.

[Exeunt Montezuma, Guyomar and Alibech.

ODMAR - Lost and undone! he had my father's voice,
And Alibech seemed pleased with her new choice:
Alas, it was not new! too late I see,
Since one she hated, that it must be me.
I feel a strange temptation in my will
To do an action, great at once and ill:
Virtue, ill treated, from my soul is fled;
I by revenge and love am wholly led:
Yet conscience would against my rage rebel—
Conscience, the foolish pride of doing well!
Sink empire, father perish, brother fall,
Revenge does more than recompence you all.
Conduct the prisoners in.

Enter Vasquez, and Pizarro.

Spaniards, you See your own deplored estate:
What dare you do to reconcile your fate?

ASQUEZ - All that despair, with courage joined, can do.

ODMAR - An easy way to victory I'll shew;
When all are buried in their sleep or joy,
I'll give you arms, burn, ravish, and destroy;
For my own share one beauty I design;
Engage your honour that she shall be mine.

PIZARRO - I gladly swear.

VASQUEZ - And I; but I request
That, in return, one, who has touched my breast,
Whose name I know not, may be given to me.

ODMAR - Spaniard, 'tis just; she's yours, whoe'er she be.

VASQUEZ - The night comes on: if fortune bless the bold,
I shall possess the beauty.

PIZARRO - I the gold. [Exeunt.

SCENE IV—A Prison

Cortez discovered bound: Almeria talking with him.

ALMERIA - I come not now your constancy to prove;
You may believe me when I say I love.

CORTEZ - You have too well instructed me before
In your intentions, to believe you more.

ALMERIA - I'm justly plagued by this your unbelief,
And am myself the cause of my own grief:
But to beg love, I cannot stoop so low;
It is enough that you my passion know:
'Tis in your choice; love me, or love me not;
I have not yet my brother's death forgot.
[Lays hold on the dagger.

CORTEZ - You menace me and court me in a breath:
Your Cupid looks as dreadfully as death.

ALMERIA - Your hopes, without, are vanished into smoke:
Your captains taken, and your armies broke.

CORTEZ - In vain you urge me with my miseries:
When fortune falls, high courages can rise;
Now should I change my love, it would appear
Not the effect of gratitude, but fear.

ALMERIA - I'll to the king, and make it my request,
Or my command, that you may be releast;
And make you judge, when I have set you free,
Who best deserves your passion, I, or she.

CORTEZ - You tempt my faith so generous a way,
As without guilt might constancy betray:
But I'm so far from meriting esteem,
That, if I judge, I must myself condemn;
Yet having given my worthless heart before,
What I must ne'er possess, I will adore:
Take my devotion then this humbler way;
Devotion is the love which heaven we pay.

[Kisses her hand.

Enter Cydaria.

CYDARIA - May I believe my eyes! what do I see!
Is this her hate to him, his love to me!
'Tis in my breast she sheaths her dagger now.
False man, is this thy faith? is this thy vow?

[To him.

CORTEZ - What words, dear saint, are these I hear you use?
What faith, what vows, are those which you accuse?

CYDARIA - More cruel than the tyger o'er his spoil;
And falser than the weeping crododile:
Can you add vanity to guilt, and take
A pride to hear the conquests, which you make?
Go, publish your renown; let it be said,
You have a woman, and that loved, betrayed.

CORTEZ - With what injustice is my faith accused!
Life, freedom, empire, I at once refused;
And would again ten thousand times for you.

ALMERIA - She'll have too great content to find him true;
And therefore, since his love is not for me,
I'll help to make my rival's misery. [Aside.
Spaniard, I never thought you false before:

[To him.

Can you at once two mistresses adore?
Keep the poor soul no longer in suspence,
Your change is such as does not need defence.

CORTEZ - Riddles like these I cannot understand.

ALMERIA - Why should you blush? she saw you kiss my hand.

CYDARIA - Fear not; I will, while your first love's denied,
Favour your shame, and turn my eyes aside;
My feeble hopes in her deserts are lost:
I neither can such power nor beauty boast:
I have no tie upon you to be true,
But that, which loosened yours, my love to you.

CORTEZ - Could you have heard my words!

CYDARIA - Alas, what needs
To hear your words, when I beheld your deeds?

CORTEZ - What shall I say? the fate of love is such,
That still it sees too little or too much.
That act of mine, which does your passion move,
Was but a mark of my respect, not love.

ALMERIA - Vex not yourself excuses to prepare:
For one, you love not, is not worth your care.

CORTEZ - Cruel Almeria, take that life you gave;
Since you but worse destroy me, while you save.

CYDARIA - No, let me die, and I'll my claim resign;
For while I live, methinks, you should be mine.

CORTEZ - The bloodiest vengeance, which she could pursue,
Would be a trifle to my loss of you.

CYDARIA - Your change was wise: for, had she been denied,
A swift revenge had followed from her pride:
You from my gentle nature had no fears,
All my revenge is only in my tears.

CORTEZ - Can you imagine I so mean could prove,
To save my life by changing of my love?

CYDARIA - Since death is that which naturally we shun,
You did no more than I, perhaps, had done.

CORTEZ - Make me not doubt, fair soul, your constancy;
You would have died for love, and so would I.

ALMERIA - You may believe him; you have seen it proved.

CORTEZ - Can I not gain belief how I have loved?
What can thy ends, malicious beauty, be:

Can he, who kill'd thy brother, live for thee?

[A noise of clashing of swords.
[Vasquez within, Indians against him.

VASQUEZ - Yield, slaves, or die; our swords shall force our way.

[Within.

INDIAN - We cannot, though o'er-powered, our trust betray.

[Within.

CORTEZ - 'Tis Vasquez's voice, he brings me liberty.

VASQUEZ - In spite of fate I'll set my general free;

[Within.

Now victory for us, the town's our own.

ALMERIA - All hopes of safety and of love are gone:
As when some dreadful thunder-clap is nigh,
The winged fire shoots swiftly through the sky,
Strikes and consumes, ere scarce it does appear,
And by the sudden ill prevents the fear:
Such is my state in this amazing woe,
It leaves no power to think, much less to do.
But shall my rival live, shall she enjoy
That love in peace, I laboured to destroy?

[Aside.

CORTEZ - Her looks grow black as a tempestuous wind;
Some raging thoughts are rolling in her mind.

ALMERIA - Rival, I must your jealousy remove,
You shall, hereafter, be at rest for love.

CYDARIA - Now you are kind.

ALMERIA - He whom you love is true:
But he shall never be possest by you.

[Draws her dagger, and runs towards her.

CORTEZ - Hold, hold, ah barbarous woman! fly, oh fly!

CYDARIA - Ah pity, pity, is no succour nigh!

CORTEZ - Run, run behind me, there you may be sure,

While I have life, I will your life secure.

[Cydaria gets behind him.

ALMERIA - On him, or thee,—light vengeance any where

[She stabs and hurts him.

What have I done? I see his blood appear!

CYDARIA - It streams, it streams from every vital part:
Was there no way but this to find his heart?

ALMERIA - Ah! cursed woman, what was my design!
This weapon's point shall mix that blood with mine!

[Goes to stab herself, and being within his reach he snatches the dagger.

CORTEZ - Now neither life nor death are in your power.

ALMERIA - Then sullenly I'll wait my fatal hour.

Enter Vasquez and Pizarro, with drawn swords.

VASQUEZ - He lives, he lives.

CORTEZ - Unfetter me with speed;
Vasquez, I see you troubled that I bleed:
But 'tis not deep, our army I can head.

VASQUEZ - You to a certain victory are led;
Your men, all armed, stand silently within:
I with your freedom did the work begin.

PIZARRO - What friends we have, and how we came so strong,
We'll softly tell you as we march along.

CORTEZ - In this safe place let me secure your fear:

[To Cydaria.

No clashing swords, no noise can enter here.
Amidst our arms as quiet you shall be,
As Halcyons brooding on a winter sea.

CYDARIA - Leave me not here alone, and full of fright,
Amidst the terrors of a dreadful night:
You judge, alas, my courage by your own;
I never durst in darkness be alone:
I beg, I throw me humbly at your feet.

CORTEZ - You must not go where you may dangers meet.
The unruly sword will no destinction make;
And beauty will not there give wounds, but take.

ALMERIA - Then stay and take me with you; tho' to be
A slave to wait upon your victory.
My heart unmoved can noise and horror bear:
Parting from you is all the death I fear.

CORTEZ - Almeria, 'tis enough I leave you free:
You neither must stay here, nor go with me.

ALMERIA - Then take my life, that will my rest restore:
'Tis all I ask, for saving yours before.

CORTEZ - That were a barbarous return of love.

ALMERIA - Yet, leaving it, you more inhuman prove.
In both extremes I some relief should find;
Oh! either hate me more, or be more kind.

CORTEZ - Life of my soul, do not my absence mourn:
But chear your heart in hopes of my return.

[To Cydaria

Your noble father's life shall be my care;
And both your brothers I'm obliged to spare.

CYDARIA - Fate makes you deaf, while I in vain implore;
My heart forebodes, I ne'er shall see you more:
I have but one request, when I am dead,
Let not my rival to your love succeed.

CORTEZ - Fate will be kinder than your fears foretell;
Farewell, my dear.

CYDARIA - A long and last farewell:
So eager to employ the cruel sword?
Can you not one, not one last look afford!

CORTEZ - I melt to womanish tears, and if I stay,
I find my love, my courage will betray;
Yon tower will keep you safe, but be so kind
To your own life, that none may entrance find.

CYDARIA - Then lead me there.—[He leads her.
For this one minute of your company,
I go, methinks, with some content to die.

[Exeunt Cortez, Vasquez, Pizarro, and Cydaria.

ALMERIA - Farewell, O too much lov'd, since lov'd in vain!
What dismal fortune does for me remain!
Night and despair my fatal footsteps guide;
That chance may give the death which he denied.

[Exit.

Cortez, Vasquez, Pizarro and Spaniards return again.

CORTEZ - All I hold dear I trust to your defence;

[To Pizarro

Guard her, and on your life, remove not hence.

[Exeunt Cortez and Vasquez.

PIZARRO - I'll venture that.
The Gods are good; I'll leave her to their care,
Steal from my post, and in the plunder share.

[Exit.

ACT V

SCENE I—A Chamber Royal, an Indian Hammock Discovered in It

Enter Odmar with soldiers, Guyomar, and Alibech bound.

ODMAR - Fate is more just than you to my desert,
And in this act you blame, heaven takes my part.

GUYOMAR - Can there be gods, and no revenge provide?

ODMAR - The gods are ever of the conquering side:
She's now my queen; the Spaniards have agreed,
I to my father's empire shall succeed.

ALIBECH - How much I crowns contemn, I let thee see,
Chusing the younger, and refusing thee.

GUYOMAR - Were she ambitious, she'd disdain to own
The pageant pomp of such a servile throne;
A throne, which thou by parricide dost gain,
And by a base submission must retain.

ALIBECH - I loved thee not before; but, Odmar, know,
That now I hate thee, and despise thee too.

ODMAR - With too much violence you crimes pursue,
Which if I acted, 'twas for love of you.
This, if it teach not love, may teach you fear:
I brought not sin so far, to stop it here.
Death in a lover's mouth would sound but ill:
But know, I either must enjoy, or kill.

ALIBECH - Bestow, base man, thy idle threats elsewhere,
My mother's daughter knows not how to fear.
Since, Guyomar, I must not be thy bride,
Death shall enjoy what is to thee denied.

ODMAR - Then take thy wish—

GUYOMAR - Hold, Odmar, hold:
My right in Alibech I will resign;
Rather than see her die, I'll see her thine.

ALIBECH - In vain thou wouldst resign, for I will be,
Even when thou leav'st me, constant still to thee:
That shall not save my life: Wilt thou appear
Fearful for her, who for herself wants fear?

ODMAR - Her love to him shows me a surer way:
I by her love her virtue must betray.—[Aside.
Since, Alibech, you are so true a wife, [To her.
'Tis in your power to save your husband's life:
The gods, by me, your love and virtue try;
For both will suffer, if you let him die.

ALIBECH - I never can believe you will proceed
To such a black, and execrable deed.

ODMAR - I only threatened you; but could not prove
So much a fool, to murder what I love:
But in his death I some advantage see:
Worse than it is I'm sure it cannot be.
If you consent, you with that gentle breath
Preserve his life: If not, behold his death.

[Holds his sword to his breast.

ALIBECH - What shall I do!

GUYOMAR - What, are your thoughts at strife
About a ransom to preserve my life?
Though to save yours I did my interest give,
Think not, when you were his, I meant to live.

ALIBECH - O let him be preserved by any way:

But name not the foul price which I must pay.

ODMAR - You would, and would not, I'll no longer stay.

[Offers again to kill him.

ALIBECH - I yield, I yield; but yet, ere I am ill,
An innocent desire I would fulfil:
With Guyomar I one chaste kiss would leave,
The first and last he ever can receive.

ODMAR - Have what you ask: That minute you agree
To my desires, your husband shall be free.
[They unbind her, she goes to her husband.

GUYOMAR - No, Alibech, we never must embrace.

[He turns from her.

Your guilty kindness why do you misplace?
'Tis meant to him, he is your private choice;
I was made yours but by the public voice.
And now you leave me with a poor pretence,
That your ill act is for my life's defence.

ALIBECH - Since there remains no other means to try,
Think I am false; I cannot see you die.

GUYOMAR - To give for me both life and honour too,
Is more, perhaps, than I could give for you.
You have done much to cure my jealousy,
But cannot perfect it unless both die!
For since both cannot live, who stays behind
Must be thought fearful, or, what's worse, unkind.

ALIBECH - I never could propose that death you chuse;
But am, like you, too jealous to refuse.

[Embracing him.

Together dying, we together show
That both did pay that faith, which both did owe.

ODMAR - It then remains I act my own design:
Have you your wills, but I will first have mine.
Assist me, soldiers—

[They go to bind her: She cries out.

Enter Vasquez, and two Spaniards.

VASQUEZ - Hold, Odmar, hold! I come in happy time
To hinder my misfortune, and your crime.

ODMAR - You ill return the kindness I have shown.

VASQUEZ - Indian, I say, desist.

ODMAR - Spaniard, be gone.

VASQUEZ - This lady I did for myself design:
Dare you attempt her honour, who is mine?

ODMAR - You're much mistaken; this is she, whom I
Did with my father's loss, and country's buy:
She, whom your promise did to me convey,
When all things else were made your common prey.
VASQUEZ - That promise made, excepted one for me;
One whom I still reserved, and this is she.

ODMAR - This is not she; you cannot be so base.

VASQUEZ - I love too deeply to mistake the face:
The vanquished must receive the victor's laws.

ODMAR - If I am vanquished, I myself am cause.

VASQUEZ - Then thank yourself for what you undergo.

ODMAR - Thus lawless might does justice overthrow.

VASQUEZ - Traitors, like you, should never justice name.

ODMAR - You owe your triumphs to that traitor's shame.
But to your general I'll my right refer.

VASQUEZ - He never will protect a ravisher:
His generous heart will soon decide our strife;
He to your brother will restore his wife.
It rests we two our claim in combat try,
And that with this fair prize the victor fly.

ODMAR - Make haste,
I cannot suffer to be long perplext;
Conquest is my first wish, and death my next.

[They fight, the Spaniards and Indians fight.

ALIBECH - The gods the wicked by themselves o'erthrow:
All fight against us now, and for us too!
[Unbinds her husband.

[The two Spaniards and three Indians kill each other, Vasquez kills Odmar, Guyomar runs to his brothers sword.

VASQUEZ - Now you are mine; my greatest foe is slain.

[To Alibech.

GUYOMAR - A greater still to vanquish does remain.

VASQUEZ - Another yet!
The wounds, I make, but sow new enemies,
Which from their blood, like earth-born brethren, rise.

GUYOMAR - Spaniard, take breath: Some respite I'll afford,
My cause is more advantage than your sword.

VASQUEZ - Thou art so brave—could it with honour be,
I'd seek thy friendship more than victory.

GUYOMAR - Friendship with him, whose hand did Odmar kill!
Base as he was, he was my brother still:
And since his blood has washed away his guilt.
Nature asks thine for that which thou hast spilt.

[They fight a little and breathe, Alibech takes up a sword and comes on.

ALIBECH - My weakness may help something in the strife.

GUYOMAR - Kill not my honour to preserve my life:

[Staying her.

Rather than by thy aid I'll conquest gain,
Without defence I poorly will be slain.

[She goes back, they fight again, Vasquez falls.

GUYOMAR - Now, Spaniard, beg thy life, and thou shalt live.

VASQUEZ - 'Twere vain to ask thee what thou canst not give;
My breath goes out, and I am now no more;
Yet her, I loved, in death I will adore. [Dies.

GUYOMAR - Come, Alibech, let us from hence remove.
This is a night of horror, not of love.
From every part I hear a dreadful noise,
The vanquished crying, and the victor's joys.
I'll to my father's aid and country's fly,
And succour both, or in their ruin die.

[Exeunt.

SCENE II—A Prison

Montezuma, Indian High Priest, bound; Pizarro, Spaniards with swords drawn, a Christian Priest.

PIZARRO - Thou hast not yet discovered all thy store.

MONTEZUMA - I neither can nor will discover more;
The gods will punish you, if they be just;
The gods will plague your sacrilegious lust.

CHRISTIAN PRIEST - Mark how this impious heathen justifies
His own false gods, and our true God denies:
How wickedly he has refused his wealth,
And hid his gold, from christian hands, by stealth:
Down with him, kill him, merit heaven thereby.

INDIAN HIGH PRIEST - Can heaven be author of such cruelty?

PIZARRO - Since neither threats nor kindness will prevail,
We must by other means your minds assail;
Fasten the engines; stretch 'em at their length,
And pull the straitened cords with all your strength.

[They fasten them to the rack, and then pull them.

MONTEZUMA - The gods, who made me once a king, shall know,
I still am worthy to continue so:
Though now the subject of your tyranny,
I'll plague you worse than you can punish me.
Know, I have gold, which you shall never find;
No pains, no tortures, shall unlock my mind.
CHRISTIAN PRIEST - Pull harder yet; he does not feel the rack.

MONTEZUMA - Pull 'till my veins break, and my sinews crack.

INDIAN HIGH PRIEST - When will you end your barbarous cruelty?
I beg not to escape, I beg to die.

MONTEZUMA - Shame on thy priesthood, that such prayers can bring!
Is it not brave, to suffer with thy king?
When monarchs suffer, gods themselves bear part;
Then well mayest thou, who but my vassal art:
I charge thee, dare not groan, nor shew one sign;
Thou at thy torments dost the least repine.

INDIAN HIGH PRIEST - You took an oath, when you received the crown,
The heavens should pour their usual blessings down;
The sun should shine, the earth its fruits produce,

And nought be wanting to your subjects' use:
Yet we with famine were opprest, and now
Must to the yoke of cruel masters bow.

MONTEZUMA - If those above, who made the world, could be
Forgetful of it, why then blamest thou me?

CHRISTIAN PRIEST - Those pains, O prince, thou sufferest now, are light
Compared to those, which, when thy soul takes flight,
Immortal, endless, thou must then endure,
Which death begins, and time can never cure.

MONTEZUMA - Thou art deceived; for whensoe'er I die,
The Sun, my father, bears my soul on high:
He lets me down a beam, and mounted there,
He draws it back, and pulls me through the air:
I in the eastern parts, and rising sky,
You in heaven's downfal, and the west must lie.

CHRISTIAN PRIEST - Fond man, by heathen ignorance misled,
Thy soul destroying when thy body's dead:
Change yet thy faith, and buy eternal rest.

INDIAN HIGH PRIEST - Die in your own, for our belief is best.

MONTEZUMA - In seeking happiness you both agree,
But in the search, the paths so different be,
That all religions with each other fight,
While only one can lead us in the right.
But till that one hath some more certain mark,
Poor human kind must wander in the dark;
And suffer pain eternally below,
For that, which here we cannot come to know.

CHRISTIAN PRIEST - That, which we worship, and which you believe,
From nature's common hand we both receive:
All, under various names, adore and love
One Power immense, which ever rules above.
Vice to abhor, and virtue to pursue,
Is both believed and taught by us and you:
But here our worship takes another way—

MONTEZUMA - Where both agree, 'tis there most safe to stay:
For what's more vain than public light to shun,
And set up tapers, while we see the sun?

CHRISTIAN PRIEST - Though nature teaches whom we should adore,
By heavenly beams we still discover more.

MONTEZUMA - Or this must be enough, or to mankind
One equal way to bliss is not designed;

For though some more may know, and some know less,
Yet all must know enough for happiness.

CHRISTIAN PRIEST - If in this middle way you still pretend
To stay, your journey never will have end.

MONTEZUMA - Howe'er, 'tis better in the midst to stay,
Than wander farther in uncertain way.

CHRISTIAN PRIEST - But we by martyrdom our faith avow.

MONTEZUMA - You do no more than I for ours do now.
To prove religion true—
If either wit or sufferings would suffice,
All faiths afford the constant and the wise:
And yet even they, by education swayed,
In age defend what infancy obeyed.

CHRISTIAN PRIEST - Since age by erring childhood is misled,
Refer yourself to our unerring head.

MONTEZUMA - Man, and not err! what reason can you give?

CHRISTIAN PRIEST - Renounce that carnal reason, and believe.

MONTEZUMA - The light of nature should I thus betray,
'Twere to wink hard, that I might see the day.

CHRISTIAN PRIEST - Condemn not yet the way you do not know;
I'll make your reason judge what way to go.

MONTEZUMA - 'Tis much too late for me new ways to take,
Who have but one short step of life to make.

PIZARRO - Increase their pains, the cords are yet too slack.

CHRISTIAN PRIEST - I must by force convert him on the rack.

INDIAN HIGH PRIEST - I faint away, and find I can no more:
Give leave, O king, I may reveal thy store,
And free myself from pains, I cannot bear.

MONTEZUMA - Think'st thou I lie on beds of roses here,
Or in a wanton bath stretched at my ease?
Die, slave, and with thee die such thoughts as these.
[High Priest turns aside, and dies.

Enter Cortez attended by Spaniards, he speaks entering.

CORTEZ - On pain of death, kill none but those who fight;
I much repent me of this bloody night:

Slaughter grows murder when it goes too far,
And makes a massacre what was a war:
Sheath all your weapons, and in silence move,
'Tis sacred here to beauty, and to love.
Ha—[Sees Montezuma
What dismal sight is this, which takes from me
All the delight, that waits on victory!

[Runs to take him off the rack.

Make haste: How now, religion, do you frown?
Haste, holy avarice, and help him down.
Ah, father, father, what do I endure

[Embracing Montezuma

To see these wounds my pity cannot cure!

MONTEZUMA - Am I so low that you should pity bring,
And give an infant's comfort to a king?
Ask these, if I have once unmanly groaned;
Or aught have done deserving to be moaned.

CORTEZ - Did I not charge, thou shouldst not stir from hence?

[To Pizarro

But martial law shall punish thy offence.
And you, [To the Christian Priest.
Who saucily teach monarchs to obey,
And the wide world in narrow cloisters sway;
Set up by kings as humble aids of power,
You that which bred you, viper-like, devour,
You enemies of crowns—

CHRISTIAN PRIEST - Come, let's away,
We but provoke his fury by our stay.

CORTEZ - If this go free, farewell that discipline,
Which did in Spanish camps severely shine:
Accursed gold, 'tis thou hast caused these crimes;
Thou turn'st our steel against thy parent climes!
And into Spain wilt fatally be brought,
Since with the price of blood thou here art bought.

[Exeunt Priest and Pizarro.

[Cortez kneels by Montezuma, and weeps.

CORTEZ - Can you forget those crimes they did commit?

MONTEZUMA - I'll do what for my dignity is fit:
Rise, sir, I'm satisfied the fault was theirs:
Trust me, you make me weep to see your tears:
Must I chear you?

CORTEZ - Ah heavens!

MONTEZUMA - You're much to blame;
Your grief is cruel, for it shows my shame,
Does my lost crown to my remembrance bring:
But weep not you, and I'll be still a king.
You have forgot, that I your death designed,
To satisfy the proud Almeria's mind:
You, who preserved my life, I doomed to die.

CORTEZ - Your love did that, and not your cruelty.

Enter a Spaniard.

SPANIARD - Prince Guyomar the combat still maintains,
Our men retreat, and he their ground regains:
But once encouraged by our general's sight,
We boldly should renew the doubtful fight.

CORTEZ - Remove not hence, you shall not long attend;

[To Montezuma.

I'll aid my soldiers, yet preserve my friend.

MONTEZUMA - Excellent man! [Exeunt Cortez, &c.
But I, by living, poorly take the way
To injure goodness, which I cannot pay.

Enter Almeria.

ALMERIA - Ruin and death run armed through every street;
And yet that fate, I seek, I cannot meet:
What guards misfortunes are and misery!
Death, that strikes all, yet seems afraid of me.

MONTEZUMA - Almeria here! Oh turn away your face!
Must you be witness too of my disgrace?

ALMERIA - I am not that Almeria whom you knew,
But want that pity I denied to you:
Your conqueror, alas, has vanquished me;
But he refuses his own victory:
While all are captives in your conquered state,
I find a wretched freedom in his hate.

MONTEZUMA - Couldst thou thy love on one who scorned thee lose?
He saw not with my eyes, who could refuse:
Him, who could prove so much unkind to thee,
I ne'er will suffer to be kind to me.

ALMERIA - I am content in death to share your fate;
And die for him I love, with him I hate.

MONTEZUMA - What shall I do in this perplexing strait!
My tortured limbs refuse to bear my weight:
[Endeavouring to walk, not being able.
I cannot go to death to set me free;
Death must be kind, and come himself to me.

ALMERIA - I've thought upon't: I have affairs below,

[Almeria musing.

Which I must needs despatch before I go:
Sir, I have found a place where you may be, [To him.
(Though not preserved) yet, like a king, die free;
The general left your daughter in the tower,
We may a while resist the Spaniards' power,
If Guyomar prevail.

MONTEZUMA - Make haste and call;
She'll hear your voice, and answer from the wall.

ALMERIA - My voice she knows and fears, but use your own;
And, to gain entrance, feign you are alone.

[Almeria steps behind.

MONTEZUMA - Cydaria!

ALMERIA - Louder.

MONTEZUMA - Daughter!

ALMERIA - Louder yet.

MONTEZUMA - Thou canst not, sure, thy father's voice forget.

[He knocks at the door, at last Cydaria looks over the balcony.

CYDARIA - Since my love went, I have been frighted so,
With dismal groans, and noises from below;
I durst not send my eyes abroad, for fear
Of seeing dangers, which I yet but hear.

MONTEZUMA - Cydaria!

CYDARIA - Sure, 'tis my father calls.

MONTEZUMA - Dear child, make haste;
All hope of succour, but from thee, is past:
As when, upon the sands, the traveller
Sees the high sea come rolling from afar,
The land grow short, he mends his weary pace,
While death behind him covers all the place:
So I, by swift misfortunes, am pursued,
Which on each other are, like waves, renewed.

CYDARIA - Are you alone?

MONTEZUMA - I am.

CYDARIA - I'll strait descend;
Heaven did you here for both our safeties send.

[Cydaria descends and opens the door, Almeria rushes betwixt with Montezuma.

CYDARIA - Almeria here! then I am lost again.

[Both thrust.

ALMERIA - Yield to my strength, you struggle but in vain.
Make haste and shut, our enemies appear.

[Cortez and Spaniards appear at the other end.

CYDARIA - Then do you enter, and let me stay here.

[As she speaks, Almeria overpowers her, thrusts her in, and shuts.

CORTEZ - Sure I both heard her voice and saw her face:
She's like a vision vanished from the place.
Too late I find my absence was too long;
My hopes grow sickly, and my fears grow strong.

[He knocks a little, then Montezuma, Cydaria, and Almeria, appear above.

ALMERIA - Look up, look up, and see if you can know
Those, whom in vain you think to find below.

CYDARIA - Look up, and see Cydaria's lost estate.

MONTEZUMA - And cast one look on Montezuma's fate.

CORTEZ - Speak not such dismal words as wound my ear;
Nor name death to me, when Cydaria's there.
Despair not, sir; who knows but conquering Spain

May part of what you lost restore again?

MONTEZUMA - No, Spaniard; know, he who, to empire born,
Lives to be less, deserves the victor's scorn:
Kings and their crowns have but one destiny:
Power is their life; when that expires, they die.

CYDARIA - What dreadful words are these!

MONTEZUMA - Name life no more;
'Tis now a torture worse than all I bore;
I'll not be bribed to suffer life, but die,
In spite of your mistaken clemency.
I was your slave, and I was used like one;
The shame continues when the pain is gone:
But I'm a king while this is in my hand—[His sword.
He wants no subjects, who can death command:
You should have tied him up, t'have conquered me;
But he's still mine, and thus he sets me free.

[Stabs himself.

CYDARIA - Oh, my dear father!

ALMERIA - When that is forced, there yet remain two more.
[The Soldiers break open the first door, and go in.
We shall have time enough to take our way,
Ere any can our fatal journey stay.

MONTEZUMA - Already mine is past: O powers divine,
Take my last thanks: no longer I repine;
I might have lived my own mishap to mourn,
While some would pity me, but more would scorn!
For pity only on fresh objects stays,
But with the tedious sight of woes decays.
Still less and less my boiling spirits flow;
And I grow stiff, as cooling metals do.
Farewell, Almeria. [Dies.

CYDARIA - He's gone, he's gone,
And leaves poor me defenceless here alone.

ALMERIA - You shall not long be so: Prepare to die,
That you may bear your father company.

CYDARIA - O name not death to me! you fright me so,
That with the fear I shall prevent the blow:
I know, your mercy's more than to destroy
A thing so young, so innocent as I.

CORTEZ - Whence can proceed thy cruel thirst of blood,

Ah, barbarous woman? Woman! that's too good,
Too mild for thee: There's pity in that name,
But thou hast lost thy pity with thy shame.

ALMERIA - Your cruel words have pierced me to the heart;
But on my rival I'll revenge my smart.

CORTEZ - Oh stay your hand; and, to redeem my fault,
I'll speak the kindest words—
That tongue e'er uttered, or that heart e'er thought.
Dear—lovely—sweet—

ALMERIA - This but offends me more;
You act your kindness on Cydaria's score.

CYDARIA - For his dear sake let me my life receive.

ALMERIA - Fool, for his sake alone you must not live:
Revenge is now my joy; he's not for me,
And I'll make sure he ne'er shall be for thee.

CYDARIA - But what's my crime?

ALMERIA - 'Tis loving where I love.

CYDARIA - Your own example does my act approve.

ALMERIA - 'Tis such a fault I never can forgive.

CYDARIA - How can I mend, unless you let me live?
I yet am tender, young, and full of fear,
And dare not die, but fain would tarry here.

CORTEZ - If blood you seek, I will my own resign:
O spare her life, and in exchange take mine!

ALMERIA - The love you shew but hastes her death the more.

CORTEZ - I'll run, and help to force the inner door.
[Is going in haste.

ALMERIA - Stay, Spaniard, stay; depart not from my eyes:
That moment that I lose your sight, she dies.
To look on you, I'll grant a short reprieve.

CORTEZ - O make your gift more full, and let her live!
I dare not go; and yet how dare I stay!
Her I would save, I murder either way.

CYDARIA - Can you be so hard-hearted to destroy
My ripening hopes, that are so near to joy?

I just approach to all I would possess:
Death only stands 'twixt me and happiness.

ALMERIA - Your father, with his life, has lost his throne:
Your country's freedom and renown is gone.
Honour requires your death; you must obey.

CYDARIA - Do you die first, and shew me then the way.

ALMERIA - Should you not follow, my revenge were lost.

CYDARIA - Then rise again, and fright me with your ghost.

ALMERIA - I will not trust to that; since death I chuse,
I'll not leave you that life which I refuse:
If death's a pain, it is not less to me;
And if 'tis nothing, 'tis no more to thee.
But hark! the noise increases from behind;
They're near, and may prevent what I designed;
Take there a rival's gift. [Stabs her.

CORTEZ - Perdition seize thee for so black a deed.

ALMERIA - Blame not an act, which did from love proceed:
I'll thus revenge thee with this fatal blow;

[Stabs herself.

Stand fair, and let my heart-blood on thee flow.

CYDARIA - Stay, life, and keep me in the cheerful light!
Death is too black, and dwells in too much night.
Thou leav'st me, life, but love supplies thy part,
And keeps me warm, by lingering in my heart:
Yet dying for him, I thy claim remove;
How dear it costs to conquer in my love!
Now strike: That thought, I hope, will arm my breast.

ALMERIA - Ah, with what differing passions am I prest!

CYDARIA - Death, when far off, did terrible appear;
But looks less dreadful as he comes more near.

ALMERIA - O rival, I have lost the power to kill;
Strength hath forsook my arm, and rage my will:
I must surmount that love which thou hast shown;
Dying for him is due to me alone.
Thy weakness shall not boast the victory,
Now thou shalt live, and dead I'll conquer thee:
Soldiers, assist me down.

[Exeunt from above, led by Soldiers, and enter both, led by Cortez.

CORTEZ - Is there no danger then? [To Cydaria.

CYDARIA - You need not fear My wound; I cannot die when you are near.

CORTEZ - You, for my sake, life to Cydaria give;

[To Almeria

And I could die for you, if you might live.

ALMERIA - Enough, I die content, now you are kind;
Killed in my limbs, reviving in my mind:
Come near, Cydaria, and forgive my crime.

[Cydaria starts back.

You need not fear my rage a second time:
I'll bathe your wounds in tears for my offence.
That hand, which made it, makes this recompence.

[Ready to join their hands.

I would have joined you, but my heart's too high:
You will, too soon, possess him when I die.

CORTEZ - She faints; O softly set her down.

ALMERIA - 'Tis past!
In thy loved bosom let me breathe my last.
Here, in this one short moment that I live,
I have whate'er the longest life could give. [Dies.

CORTEZ - Farewell, thou generous maid: Even victory,
Glad as it is, must lend some tears to thee;
Many I dare not shed, lest you believe [To Cydaria
I joy in you less than for her I grieve.

CYDARIA - But are you sure she's dead?
I must embrace you fast, before I know,
Whether my life be yet secure, or no:
Some other hour I will to tears allow,
But, having you, can shew no sorrow now.

Enter Guyomar and Alibech bound, with Soldiers.

CORTEZ - Prince Guyomar in bonds! O friendship's shame!
It makes me blush to own a victor's name.

[Unbinds him, Cydaria, Alibech.

CYDARIA - See, Alibech, Almeria lies there;
But do not think 'twas I that murdered her.

[Alibech kneels, and kisses her dead sister.

CORTEZ - Live, and enjoy more than your conqueror:

[To Guyomar.

Take all my love, and share in all my power.

GUYOMAR - Think me not proudly rude, if I forsake
Those gifts I cannot with my honour take:
I for my country fought, and would again,
Had I yet left a country to maintain:
But since the gods decreed it otherwise,
I never will on its dear ruins rise.

ALIBECH - Of all your goodness leaves to our dispose,
Our liberty's the only gift we chuse:
Absence alone can make our sorrows less;
And not to see what we can ne'er redress.

GUYOMAR - Northward, beyond the mountains, we will go,
Where rocks lie covered with eternal snow,
Thin herbage in the plains and fruitless fields,
The sand no gold, the mine no silver yields:
There love and freedom we'll in peace enjoy;
No Spaniards will that colony destroy.
We to ourselves will all our wishes grant;
And, nothing coveting, can nothing want.

CORTEZ - First your great father's funeral pomp provide:
That done, in peace your generous exiles guide;
While I loud thanks pay to the powers above,
Thus doubly blest, with conquest, and with love.

[Exeunt.

EPILOGUE

BY A MERCURY

To all and singular in this full meeting,
Ladies and gallants, Phoebus sends ye greeting.
To all his sons, by whate'er title known,
Whether of court, or coffee-house, or town;
From his most mighty sons, whose confidence

Is placed in lofty sound, and humble sense,
Even to his little infants of the time,
Who write new songs, and trust in tune and rhyme:
Be't known, that Phoebus (being daily grieved
To see good plays condemned, and bad received)
Ordains, your judgment upon every cause,
Henceforth, be limited by wholesome laws.
He first thinks fit no sonnetteer advance
His censure, farther than the song or dance.
Your wit burlesque may one step higher climb,
And in his sphere may judge all doggrel rhyme:
All proves, and moves, and loves, and honours too;
All that appears high sense, and scarce is low.
As for the coffee-wits, he says not much;
Their proper business is to damn the Dutch:
For the great dons of wit—
Phoebus gives them full privilege alone,
To damn all others, and cry up their own.
Last, for the ladies, 'tis Apollo's will,
They should have power to save, but not to kill:
For love and he long since have thought it fit,
Wit live by beauty, beauty reign by wit.

John Dryden – A Short Biography

John Dryden was born on August 9th, 1631 in the village rectory of Aldwincle near Thrapston in Northamptonshire, where his maternal grandfather was Rector of All Saints Church.

Dryden was the eldest of fourteen children born to Erasmus Dryden and wife Mary Pickering, paternal grandson of Sir Erasmus Dryden, 1st Baronet (1553–1632) and wife Frances Wilkes, Puritan landowning gentry who supported the Puritan cause and Parliament.

As a boy Dryden lived in the nearby village of Titchmarsh, Northamptonshire where it is probable that he received his first education.

In 1644 he was sent to Westminster School as a King's Scholar where his headmaster was Dr. Richard Busby, a charismatic teacher but severe disciplinarian. Having recently been re-founded by Elizabeth I, Westminster now embraced a very different religious and political spirit encouraging royalism and high Anglicanism but as a humanist public school, it maintained a curriculum which trained pupils in the art of rhetoric and the presentation of arguments for both sides of a given issue. This skill would remain with Dryden and influence his later writing and thinking, as much of it displays these dialectical patterns.

His first published poem, whilst still at Westminster, was an elegy with a strong royalist flavour on the death of his schoolmate Henry, Lord Hastings from smallpox, and alludes to the execution of King Charles I, which took place on January 30th, 1649.

In 1650 Dryden was ready for University and travelled to Trinity College, Cambridge. Dryden's undergraduate years would almost certainly have followed the standard curriculum of classics, rhetoric, and mathematics.

Dryden obtained his BA in 1654, graduating top of the list for Trinity that year.

However family tragedy struck in June of the same year when Dryden's father died, leaving him some land which generated a small income, but not enough to live on.

Returning to London during The Protectorate, Dryden now obtained work with Cromwell's Secretary of State, John Thurloe. This may have been the result of influence exercised on his behalf by his cousin the Lord Chamberlain, Sir Gilbert Pickering.

At Cromwell's funeral on 23 November 1658 Dryden was in the company of the Puritan poets John Milton and Andrew Marvell. The setting was to be a sea change in English history. From Republic to Monarchy and from one set of lauded poets to what would soon become the Age of Dryden.

The start began later that year when Dryden published the first of his great poems, Heroic Stanzas (1658), a eulogy on Cromwell's death which is necessarily cautious and prudent in its emotional display.

With the Restoration of the Monarchy in 1660 Dryden celebrated in verse with Astraea Redux, an authentic royalist panegyric. In this work the interregnum is illustrated as a time of anarchy, and Charles is seen as the restorer of peace and order.

With the king now established Dryden moved quickly to place himself as the leading poet and critic of his day and transferred his allegiances to the new government.

Along with Astraea Redux, Dryden welcomed the new regime with two more panegyrics: To His Sacred Majesty: A Panegyric on his Coronation (1662) and To My Lord Chancellor (1662).

These panegyrics are occasional and written to celebrate events. Thus they are written for the nation rather than the self, but these and others put him in good standing for his eventual appointment as Poet Laureate, where a number of event poems would be required each year and speaking for the Nation and to the Nation would be the first order of duty.

These poems suggest that Dryden was looking to court a possible patron which would have given him an income and time to explore his creative ideas but no, his path instead would be to make a living in writing for publishers, not for the aristocracy, and thus ultimately for the reading public.

In November 1662 Dryden was proposed for membership in the Royal Society, and he was elected an early fellow. However, his inactivity and non payment of dues led to his expulsion in 1666.

On December 1st, 1663 Dryden married the Royalist sister of Sir Robert Howard—Lady Elizabeth Howard (died 1714). The marriage was at St. Swithin's, London, and the consent of the parents is noted on the license, though Lady Elizabeth was then about twenty-five. She was the object of some scandals, well or ill founded; it was said that Dryden had been bullied into the marriage by her brothers. A small estate in Wiltshire was settled upon them by her father. The lady's intellect and temper were apparently not good; her husband was treated as an inferior by those of her social status.

Dryden's works occasionally contain outbursts against the married state but also celebrations of the same. Little else is known of the intimate side of his marriage.

Both Dryden and his wife were warmly attached to their children. They had three sons: Charles (1666–1704), John (1668–1701), and Erasmus Henry (1669–1710). Lady Elizabeth Dryden survived her husband, but went insane soon after his death and died in 1714.

With the re-opening of the theatres after the Puritan ban, Dryden began to also write plays. His first play, The Wild Gallant, appeared in 1663 but was not successful. From 1668 on he was contracted to produce three plays a year for the King's Company, in which he became a shareholder. During the 1660s and '70s, theatrical writing was his main source of income. He led the way in Restoration comedy, his best-known works being Marriage à la Mode (1672), as well as heroic tragedy and regular tragedy, in which his greatest success was All for Love (1678). Dryden was never fully satisfied with his theatrical writings and frequently suggested that his talents were wasted on unworthy audiences.

Certainly therefore fame as a poet looked more rewarding. In 1667, around the same time his dramatic career began, he published Annus Mirabilis, a lengthy historical poem which described the English defeat of the Dutch naval fleet and the Great Fire of London in 1666. It was a modern epic in pentameter quatrains that established him as the pre-eminent poet of his generation, and was crucial in his attaining the posts of Poet Laureate (1668) and then historiographer royal (1670).

When the Great Plague of London closed the theatres in 1665 Dryden retreated to Wiltshire where he wrote Of Dramatick Poesie (1668), arguably the best of his unsystematic prefaces and essays. Dryden constantly defended his own literary practice, and Of Dramatick Poesie, the longest of his critical works, takes the form of a dialogue in which four characters—each based on a prominent contemporary, with Dryden himself as 'Neander'—debate the merits of classical, French and English drama.

He felt strongly about the relation of the poet to tradition and the creative process, and his heroic play Aureng-zebe (1675) has a prologue which denounces the use of rhyme in serious drama. His play All for Love (1678) was written in blank verse, and was to immediately follow Aureng-Zebe.

On December 18th, 1679 he was attacked in Rose Alley near his home in Covent Garden by thugs hired by fellow poet, John Wilmot, 2nd Earl of Rochester, with whom he had a long-standing conflict. Wilmot was constantly in and out of favour with the King and his own poetry was often bawdy, lewd, even obscene and made fun of the King who would often exile him from Court.

Dryden's greatest achievements were in satiric verse: the mock-heroic Mac Flecknoe, a more personal product of his Laureate years, was a lampoon circulated in manuscript and an attack on the playwright Thomas Shadwell. Dryden's main goal in the work is to "satirize Shadwell, ostensibly for his offenses against literature but more immediately we may suppose for his habitual badgering of him on the stage and in print." It is not a belittling form of satire, but rather one which makes his object great in ways which are unexpected, transferring the ridiculous into poetry. This line of satire continued with Absalom and Achitophel (1681) and The Medal (1682). Other major works from this period are the religious poems Religio Laici (1682), written from the position of a member of the Church of England; his 1683 edition of Plutarch's Lives, translated From the Greek by Several Hands in which he introduced the word biography to English readers; and The Hind and the Panther, (1687) which celebrates his conversion to Roman Catholicism.

He wrote Britannia Rediviva celebrating the birth of a son and heir to the Catholic King and Queen on June 10th, 1688. When later in the same year James II was deposed in the Glorious Revolution, Dryden's refusal to take the oaths of allegiance to the new monarchs, William and Mary, which left him out of favour at court and he had to leave his post as Poet Laureate. Thomas Shadwell, his despised rival, succeeded him. Dryden, England's greatest literary figure, was now forced to give up his public offices and live by the proceeds of his pen alone.

Dryden was an excellent translator with his own style which brought the ire of many critics. Many felt he would embellish or expand anything he felt short or curt. Dryden did not feel such expansion was a fault, arguing that as Latin is a naturally concise language it cannot be duly represented by a comparable number of words in the much larger English vocabulary. He continued with his task of translating works by Horace, Juvenal, Ovid, Lucretius, and Theocritus, a task which he found far more satisfying than writing for the stage.

In 1694 he began work on what would be his most ambitious and defining work as translator, The Works of Virgil (1697), which was published by subscription. The publication of the translation of Virgil was a national event and brought Dryden the sum of £1,400.

His final translations appeared in the volume Fables Ancient and Modern (1700), a series of episodes from Homer, Ovid, and Boccaccio, as well as modernised adaptations from Geoffrey Chaucer interspersed with Dryden's own poems. As a translator, he made great literary works in the older languages available to readers of English.

John Dryden died on May 12th, 1700, and was initially buried in St. Anne's cemetery in Soho, before being exhumed and reburied in Westminster Abbey ten days later. He was the subject of poetic eulogies, such as Luctus Brittannici: or the Tears of the British Muses; for the Death of John Dryden, Esq. (London, 1700), and The Nine Muses.

He is seen as dominating the literary life of Restoration England to such a point that the period came to be known in literary circles as the Age of Dryden. Walter Scott called him "Glorious John."

Dryden was the dominant literary figure and influence of his age. He established the heroic couplet as a standard form of English poetry by writing successful satires, religious pieces, fables, epigrams, compliments, prologues, and plays with it; he also introduced the alexandrine and triplet into the form. In his poems, translations, and criticism, he established a poetic diction appropriate to the heroic couplet—Auden referred to him as "the master of the middle style"—that was a model for his contemporaries and for much of the 18th century. The considerable loss felt by the English literary community at his death was evident in the elegies written about him. Dryden's heroic couplet went on to become the dominant poetic form of the 18th century.

What Dryden achieved in his poetry was neither the emotional excitement of the early nineteenth-century romantics nor the intellectual complexities of the metaphysicals. Although he uses formal structures such as heroic couplets, he tried to recreate the natural rhythm of speech, and he knew that different subjects need different kinds of verse. In his preface to Religio Laici he says that "the expressions of a poem designed purely for instruction ought to be plain and natural, yet majestic... The florid, elevated and figurative way is for the passions; for (these) are begotten in the soul by showing the objects out of their true proportion.... A man is to be cheated into passion, but to be reasoned into truth."

Perhaps the following illustrates Dryden and his life—"The way I have taken, is not so streight as Metaphrase, nor so loose as Paraphrase: Some things too I have omitted, and sometimes added of my own. Yet the omissions I hope, are but of Circumstances, and such as wou'd have no grace in English; and the Addition, I also hope, are easily deduc'd from Virgil's Sense. They will seem (at least I have the Vanity to think so), not struck into him, but growing out of him".

John Dryden – A Concise Bibliography

Astraea Redux, 1660
The Wild Gallant (comedy), 1663
The Indian Emperour (tragedy), 1665
Annus Mirabilis (poem), 1667
The Enchanted Island (comedy), 1667, with William D'Avenant from Shakespeare's The Tempest
Secret Love, or The Maiden Queen, 1667
An Essay of Dramatick Poesie, 1668
An Evening's Love (comedy), 1668
Tyrannick Love (tragedy), 1669
The Conquest of Granada, 1670
The Assignation, or Love in a Nunnery, 1672
Marriage à la mode, 1672
Amboyna, or the Cruelties of the Dutch to the English Merchants, 1673
The Mistaken Husband (comedy), 1674
Aureng-zebe, 1675
All for Love, 1678
Oedipus (heroic drama), 1679, an adaptation with Nathaniel Lee of Sophocles' Oedipus
Absalom and Achitophel, 1681
The Spanish Fryar, 1681
Mac Flecknoe, 1682
The Medal, 1682
Religio Laici, 1682
To the Memory of Mr. Oldham, 1684
Threnodia Augustalis, 1685
The Hind and the Panther, 1687
A Song for St. Cecilia's Day, 1687
Britannia Rediviva, 1688, written to mark the birth of a Prince of Wales.
Amphitryon, 1690
Don Sebastian (play), 1690
Creator Spirit, by whose aid, 1690. Translation of Rabanus Maurus' Veni Creator Spiritus
King Arthur, 1691
Cleomenes, 1692
The Art of Satire, 1693
Love Triumphant, 1694
The Works of Virgil, 1697
Alexander's Feast, 1697
Fables, Ancient and Modern, 1700

www.ingramcontent.com/pod-product-compliance
Lightning Source LLC
Chambersburg PA
CBHW060135050426
42448CB00010B/2128